ORLAND PARK PUBLIC LIBRARY

W9-BSS-132

DEMCO

Modern Critical Interpretations

William Shakespeare's The Taming of the Shrew

Modern Critical Interpretations

The Oresteia
Beowulf
The General Prologue to The Canterbury Tales
The Pardoner's Tale
The Knight's Tale
The Divine Comedy
Exodus
Genesis
The Gospels
The Iliad
The Book of Job
Volpone
Doctor Faustus
The Revelation of St. John the Divine
The Song of Songs
Oedipus Rex
The Aeneid
The Duchess of Malfi
Antony and Cleopatra
As You Like It
Coriolanus
Hamlet
Henry IV, Part I
Henry IV, Part II
Henry V
Julius Caesar
King Lear
Macbeth
Measure for Measure
The Merchant of Venice
A Midsummer Night's Dream
Much Ado About Nothing
Othello
Richard II
Richard III
The Sonnets
Taming of the Shrew
The Tempest
Twelfth Night
The Winter's Tale
Emma
Mansfield Park
Pride and Prejudice
The Life of Samuel Johnson
Moll Flanders
Robinson Crusoe
Tom Jones
The Beggar's Opera
Gray's Elegy
Paradise Lost
The Rape of the Lock
Tristram Shandy
Gulliver's Travels
Evelina
The Marriage of Heaven and Hell
Songs of Innocence and Experience
Jane Eyre
Wuthering Heights
Don Juan
The Rime of the Ancient Mariner
Bleak House
David Copperfield
Hard Times
A Tale of Two Cities
Middlemarch
The Mill on the Floss
Jude the Obscure
The Mayor of Casterbridge
The Return of the Native
Tess of the D'Urbervilles
The Odes of Keats
Frankenstein
Vanity Fair
Barchester Towers
The Prelude
The Red Badge of Courage
The Scarlet Letter
The Ambassadors
Daisy Miller, The Turn of the Screw, and Other Tales
The Portrait of a Lady
Billy Budd, Benito Cereno, Bartleby the Scrivener, and Other Tales
Moby-Dick
The Tales of Poe
Walden
Adventures of Huckleberry Finn
The Life of Frederick Douglass
Heart of Darkness
Lord Jim
Nostromo
A Passage to India
Dubliners
A Portrait of the Artist as a Young Man
Ulysses
Kim
The Rainbow
Sons and Lovers
Women in Love
1984
Major Barbara
Man and Superman
Pygmalion
St. Joan
The Playboy of the Western World
The Importance of Being Earnest
Mrs. Dalloway
To the Lighthouse
My Antonia
An American Tragedy
Murder in the Cathedral
The Waste Land
Absalom, Absalom!
Light in August
Sanctuary
The Sound and the Fury
The Great Gatsby
A Farewell to Arms
The Sun Also Rises
Arrowsmith
Lolita
The Iceman Cometh
Long Day's Journey Into Night
The Grapes of Wrath
Miss Lonelyhearts
The Glass Menagerie
A Streetcar Named Desire
Their Eyes Were Watching God
Native Son
Waiting for Godot
Herzog
All My Sons
Death of a Salesman
Gravity's Rainbow
All the King's Men
The Left Hand of Darkness
The Brothers Karamazov
Crime and Punishment
Madame Bovary
The Interpretation of Dreams
The Castle
The Metamorphosis
The Trial
Man's Fate
The Magic Mountain
Montaigne's Essays
Remembrance of Things Past
The Red and the Black
Anna Karenina
War and Peace

These and other titles in preparation

Modern Critical Interpretations

William Shakespeare's

The Taming of the Shrew

Edited and with an introduction by

Harold Bloom

Sterling Professor of the Humanities

Yale University

Chelsea House Publishers ◊ 1988

NEW YORK ◊ NEW HAVEN ◊ PHILADELPHIA

Printed and bound in the United States of America

10 9 8 7 6 5 4 3 2 1

∞ The paper used in this publication meets the minimum requirements of the American National Standard for Permanence of Paper for Printed Library Materials, Z39.48-1984.

Library of Congress Cataloging-in-Publication Data
William Shakespeare's The taming of the shrew / edited and with an introduction by Harold Bloom.
p. cm.—(Modern critical interpretations)
Bibliography: p.
Includes index.
Summary: A collection of eight critical essays on the Shakespeare comedy, arranged in chronological order of their original publication.
ISBN 0-87754-939-7 (alk. paper): $19.95
1. Shakespeare, William, 1564–1616. Taming of the shrew.
[1. Shakespeare, William, 1564–1616. Taming of the shrew.
2. English literature—History and criticism.] I. Bloom, Harold.
II. Series.
PR2832.W54 1988 87-22188
822.3′3—dc19 CIP
AC

Contents

Editor's Note / vii

Introduction / 1
HAROLD BLOOM

Dream and Structure: *The Taming of the Shrew* / 5
MARJORIE B. GARBER

Patriarchy and Play in *The Taming of the Shrew* / 13
MARIANNE L. NOVY

"Kate of Kate Hall" / 29
RUTH NEVO

Coming of Age: Marriage and Manhood in *The Taming of the Shrew* / 41
COPPÉLIA KAHN

Horses and Hermaphrodites: Metamorphoses in *The Taming of the Shrew* / 53
JEANNE ADDISON ROBERTS

The Taming of the Shrew: The Bourgeoisie in Love / 65
CAROL F. HEFFERNAN

Charisma, Coercion, and Comic Form in *The Taming of the Shrew* / 79
RICHARD A. BURT

The Turn of the Shrew / 93
JOEL FINEMAN

Chronology / 115

Contributors / 117

Bibliography / 119

Acknowledgments / 123

Index / 125

Editor's Note

This book gathers together a representative selection of the best modern critical interpretations of Shakespeare's comedy *The Taming of the Shrew*. The critical essays are reprinted here in the chronological order of their original publication. I am grateful to Cornelia Pearsall and Paul Barickman for their assistance in editing this volume.

My introduction finds in the mutually violent expressionism of Kate and Petruchio that they are made for one another, and raises again the peculiar question of the play's induction. Marjorie B. Garber begins the chronological sequence of criticism by analyzing the induction to the Kate-Petruchio plot, since both Sly's dream and the lovers' relationship rely upon imagery of transformation and metamorphosis.

In Marianne L. Novy's reading, the game element in the comedy establishes a protected space where individuality and marriage, energy and form, can exist together without the fears of patriarchal violence and feminine resentment. Ruth Nevo argues that *The Taming of the Shrew* is a "psychodrama," in which Petruchio comically "cures" Kate by appealing to her intellect, since his absurd tantrums parody her own irregular behavior. Very different in her views, Coppélia Kahn is not satisfied with such comic playfulness, and instead insists that Shakespeare's profound insight is to "make the taming mirror the threat to manhood hidden in marriage."

Jeanne Addison Roberts reads the play in terms of the romance convention of metamorphosis and asserts that Shakespeare reverses the Ovidian mode of transformation, since Kate and Petruchio humanize one another. Relying upon seventeenth-century marriage manuals, Carol F. Heffernan sees Kate and Petruchio as rising above the bourgeois values that, then and now, took the world of marriage as a business.

Richard A. Burt argues that *The Taming of the Shrew* does not resolve conflicts, but rather manages and controls them so as to reinforce social norms. In this volume's final essay, Joel Fineman sets Kate's figurative and feminine language against Petruchio's more literal and supposedly masculine mode and tries to establish that Kate's subversive rhetoric ironically works so as to help strengthen patriarchal dominance.

Introduction

The Taming of the Shrew, when acted, seems almost the simplest of performance pieces, a fine farce in an immemorial tradition of male supremacy. Well before the advent of feminist criticism of Shakespeare, Harold Goddard declined to accept such an interpretation:

> *Richard III* proves that *double-entendre* was a passion of the youthful Shakespeare, and both *The Two Gentlemen of Verona* and *Love's Labor's Lost* illustrate the fact that he was fond of under- and over-meanings he could not have expected his audience as a whole to get. But it is *The Taming of the Shrew* that is possibly the most striking example among his early works of his love of so contriving a play that it should mean, to those who might choose to take it so, the precise opposite of what he knew it would mean to the multitude. For surely the most psychologically sound as well as the most delightful way of taking *The Taming of the Shrew* is the topsy-turvy one. Kate, in that case, is no shrew at all except in the most superficial sense. Bianca, on the other hand, is just what her sister is supposed to be. And the play ends with the prospect that Kate is going to be more nearly the tamer than the tamed, Petruchio more nearly the tamed than the tamer, though his wife naturally will keep the true situation under cover. So taken, the play is an early version of *What Every Woman Knows*—what every woman knows being, of course, that the woman can lord it over the man so long as she allows him to think he is lording it over her. This interpretation has the advantage of bringing the play into line with all the other Comedies in which Shakespeare gives a distinct edge to his heroine. Otherwise it is an unaccountable exception and regresses to the wholly un-Shakespearean doctrine of male superiority, a view which there is not the slightest evidence elsewhere Shakespeare ever held.

In Goddard's reading, the Christopher Sly induction is an intentional analogue to the subtle gulling of Petruchio by Kate:

> In the Induction to *The Taming of the Shrew*, Christopher Sly the tinker, drunk with ale, is persuaded that he is a great lord who has been the victim of an unfortunate lunacy. Petruchio, in the play which Sly witnesses (when he is not asleep), is likewise persuaded that he is a great lord—over his wife. Sly is obviously in for a rude awakening when he discovers that he is nothing but a tinker after all. Now Petruchio is a bit intoxicated himself—who can deny it?—whether with pride, love, or avarice, or some mixture of the three. Is it possible that he too is in for an awakening? Or, if Kate does not let it come to that, that *we* at least are supposed to see that he is not as great a lord over his wife as he imagined? The Induction and the play, taken together, do not allow us to evade these questions. Can anyone be so naïve as to fancy that Shakespeare did not contrive his Induction for the express purpose of forcing them on us? Either the cases of Sly and Petruchio are alike or they are diametrically opposite. Can there be much doubt which was intended by a poet who is so given to pointing out analogies between lovers and drunkards, between lovers and lunatics? Here surely is reason enough for Shakespeare not to show us Sly at the end when he no longer thinks himself a lord. It would be altogether too much like explaining the joke, like solving the equation and labeling the result ANSWER. Shakespeare wants us to find things for ourselves. And in this case in particular: why explain what is as clear, when you see it, as was Poe's Purloined Letter, which was skilfully concealed precisely because it was in such plain sight all the time?

This is consonant with Northrop Frye's observation that Kate in act 5 is engaged in much the same occupation as in act 1, getting back at Bianca for being the favorite (and spoiled) daughter, except that Kate, schooled by her husband, now has social convention on her side against Bianca. And yet the most celebrated of Kate's speeches remains a permanent scandal:

> KATHERINA: Fie, fie, unknit that threat'ning unkind brow,
> And dart not scornful glances from those eyes,
> To wound thy lord, thy king, thy governor.
> It blots thy beauty, as frosts do bite the meads,
> Confounds thy fame, as whirlwinds shake fair buds,
> And in no sense is meet or amiable.

A woman mov'd is like a fountain troubled,
Muddy, ill-seeming, thick, bereft of beauty,
And while it is so, none so dry or thirsty
Will deign to sip, or touch one drop of it.
Thy husband is thy lord, thy life, thy keeper,
Thy head, thy sovereign; one that cares for thee,
And for thy maintenance; commits his body
To painful labor, both by sea and land;
To watch the night in storms, the day in cold,
Whilst thou li'st warm at home, secure and safe;
And craves no other tribute at thy hands
But love, fair looks, and true obedience—
Too little payment for so great a debt.
Such duty as the subject owes the prince,
Even such a woman oweth to her husband;
And when she is froward, peevish, sullen, sour,
And not obedient to his honest will,
What is she but a foul contending rebel,
And graceless traitor to her loving lord?
I am asham'd that women are so simple
To offer war where they should kneel for peace,
Or seek for rule, supremacy, and sway,
When they are bound to serve, love, and obey.
Why are our bodies soft, and weak, and smooth,
Unapt to toil and trouble in the world,
But that our soft conditions, and our hearts,
Should well agree with our external parts?
Come, come, you froward and unable worms!
My mind hath been as big as one of yours,
My heart as great, my reason haply more,
To bandy word for word and frown for frown;
But now I see our lances are but straws,
Our strength as weak, our weakness past compare,
That seeming to be most which we indeed least are.
Then vail your stomachs, for it is no boot,
And place your hands below your husband's foot;
In token of which duty, if he please,
My hand is ready, may it do him ease.

Unlike John Milton's "He for God only, she for God in him," I rather doubt that any audience ever could have taken this to heart. A good actress can do marvelous things with: "I am asham'd that women are so simple." The clearest representational truth of *The Taming of the Shrew* is that Kate and Petruchio, both violent expressionists, were made for one another, and doubtless are likelier to live happily ever after than any other married couple in Shakespeare. If you had the Bianca-doting Baptista for a father, and you were Kate, then the amiable ruffian Petruchio would become an ideal, indeed an over-determined match.

That still leaves the puzzle of the induction, with the curious status it assigns to the Kate-Petruchio agon as a play-within-a-play or rather farce-within-a-farce. Brilliant as the induction is, it performs strangely in our mobile society, where class distinctions hardly are as they are in England now, or were in England then. Goddard may have been imaginatively correct in analogizing Sly's delusion and Petruchio's (if he is deluded), but socially the analogy cannot hold. Petruchio and Kate are in the same social class, but the drunken Sly is indeed lunatic when he accepts the deceit practiced upon him. Shakespeare's meanings are necessarily ours, but his social judgments remain those of another nation, at another time.

Dream and Structure: *The Taming of the Shrew*

Marjorie B. Garber

The "flatt'ring dream" (Ind.1.44) of noble birth, which is devised as a joke upon Christopher Sly, is a framing device in *The Taming of the Shrew*, permitting the story of the "taming" itself to be presented as a play-within-a-play. Such an induction is not uncommon in the plays of the period: the ghost of Don Andrea in Kyd's *Spanish Tragedy* (1584–88) is explicitly invited by Revenge to "serve for Chorus" (1.1.91) as the play unfolds, and the induction written by Webster for Marston's *Malcontent* (1604) places the actors of the King's Men in their own persons on the stage. In these cases, however, the use of the introductory scene is different from that in *The Shrew*; Andrea has played a principal part in the circumstances surrounding the *Tragedy*, while the *Malcontent* induction is a way of explaining the company's pirating of Marston's play. *The Shrew*'s induction is both longer and more elaborate than either of these (it introduces ten characters who never again appear), and its personages are related neither to the main action nor to the circumstances of production. Sly's dream is in fact more of a play-within-a-play than the inductions of the *Tragedy* or the *Malcontent*, and the events it contains are connected to the Kate-Petruchio plot by analogy. The metaphor of dream, like the stage metaphor, presents the audience with the problem of comparative realities and juxtaposes a simple or "low" illusion with the more courtly illusions of the taming plot itself.

The Shrew's induction owes its existence, at least in part, to identifiable sources and analogues. Its ultimate source is a story in the *Arabian Nights*,

From *Dream in Shakespeare: From Metaphor to Metamorphosis.* Yale University Press, 1974.

"The Sleeper Awakened," which made its way to England in three known forms: a letter from Juan Luis Vives to Francis, Duke of Béjar; a collection of stories assembled by Richard Edwards and published in 1570, now lost; and a story in the *De rebus burgundicis* of Heuterus (1584). The Heuterus version alludes to a comedy to be presented to the gulled sleeper and is thus the most likely actual source. None of the versions, however, drop the framing device as Shakespeare does; in all of them the prologue is balanced by an epilogue in which the effect of the dream on the sleeper is made clear. This is also the case in the anonymous *The Taming of a Shrew, The Shrew*'s most celebrated analogue. The omission of the epilogue-frame is thus an important characteristic of Shakespeare's version of the dream; it marks the story's transformation from the narrative to the dramatic mode. The symmetry of prologue-epilogue is pleasing in a tale, but—as Shakespeare may have reasoned—less feasible in a comedy, where a return to the frame might constitute an awkward anticlimax. Similarly, as has been frequently suggested, the induction as it stands provides a thematic parallel for the later action: Sly's acceptance of a new personality—after some initial resistance—foreshadows Kate's own. Contrary arguments have been advanced by some scholars to suggest either (1) a "lost" epilogue, or (2) a flaw in the play's construction because of the lack of one; by and large these contentions are merely the inverse of the others (an epilogue could be climactic rather than anticlimactic; the thematic parallel was meant to operate by contrast, when Sly loses his new identity at the close) and seem more conjectural than persuasive. Robert B. Heilman's contention that "surely most readers feel spontaneously that . . . something is left uncomfortably hanging" seems to take insufficient note of the difference between reading a play and watching one (*The Complete Signet Classic Shakespeare*).

In any case, the formal device of the induction has a considerable effect upon the play as a whole, and its importance is closely linked with the fact that it purports to tell a dream. The frame performs the important tasks of distancing the later action and of insuring a lightness of tone—significant contributions in view of the real abuse to which Kate is subjected by Petruchio. Its most important single advantage, however, is the immediacy with which it establishes the deliberate metaphorical ambiguity of reality and illusion. This is a role which we are accustomed to ascribe to the play metaphor, and the play metaphor is in some sense operative here. Because of its inherently formal and concrete character, however—*The Shrew* takes place upon a stage, and the recumbent Sly is presumably visible on the upper stage while the main plot unfolds upon the lower—the play metaphor has limitations. Though we may suspend our awareness of varying planes of reality in drama, we can never wholly escape it: Sly is always present upon the upper stage, Theseus and Hippolyta comment throughout the "Pyramus and Thisby" play, Prospero summons and interrupts the pageant of the nymphs. Even "All the world's a stage" and "O what a rogue and peasant slave am I" are in a real sense set pieces, calling attention to the remarkable circumstance of a player on a stage comparing himself extensively to a player of a player.

By comparison, dream—and Sly's dream—escapes these limitations of structure. The content of the dream, like the content of the play-within-a-play, can be measured against the play of which it is a part: in just this way, commentators remark the similarity in theme between Sly's change from beggar to lord and Kate's from shrew to wife. But at the same time something more subtle is achieved by the suggestion made to Sly that he has been dreaming. The "dream" to which the lord and his servants refer is Sly's conviction that he is a tinker named Christopher Sly. Thus, what they call his dream is actually the literal truth, while the "truth" they persuade him of is fictive. When Sly wonders aloud, "Or do I dream? Or have I dreamed till now?" (Ind.2.69), he states the general case of the problem of illusion. His own problem is concrete: he suspects that he has been awake and is now dreaming, while the servingmen attempt to persuade him that the opposite is the case. We know—or think we know—which judgment is correct, and thus Sly's pragmatic solution,

> I smell sweet savors and I feel soft things,
> Upon my life, I am a lord indeed
> And not a tinker nor Christopher Sly
> (Ind.2.71–73)

strikes us as comic, while it permits a continued play upon the interchanged terms: "These fifteen years you have been in a dream / Or when you waked so waked as if you slept" (ll. 79–80). But in the later plays, and particularly in the romances, this rhetorical and formal interchange, which is in Sly's case simple confusion, becomes a serious interpenetration of planes. When Miranda says of her memory of Milan that it is "rather like a dream than an assurance" (*The Tempest* 1.2.45), or when Leontes tells Hermione that "your actions are my dreams" (*The Winter's Tale* 3.2.80), a much more highly refined version of the same handy-dandy is at work. The extremely formal, local, and concrete use of the dream figure in *The Shrew* thus provides a starting point of sorts. It is largely device in *The Shrew*; in later plays it will become part of the dream world of transformation.

At the moment when the drunken Sly is first discovered onstage by a lord and his huntsmen, the lord exclaims:

> O monstrous beast, how like a swine he lies!
> Grim death, how foul and loathsome is thine image!
> (Ind.1.34–35)

Although they are conventional epithets, terms like "beast" and "swine" immediately establish a line of significant imagery with which the induction—like the play as a whole—will be much concerned: the imagery of transformation or metamorphosis. The entire "supposes" plot based on Gascoigne turns on change of guise—Lucentio as a tutor, Tranio as Lucentio, the pedant as Vincentio, as well as the more symbolic changes undergone by Kate and Petruchio. With superb economy Shakespeare introduces the theme at once in a casual, almost accidental way. For part of the effectiveness of the "beast-swine" terminology lies precisely in the fact of its conventionalism: the imagery enters the play in the form of metaphors so common as to lack strong metaphorical force; yet as the play progresses this seeming convention becomes more and more relevant and particular. The lord's next lines point out the chain of development:

> Sirs, I will practice on this drunken man.
> What think you, if he were conveyed to bed,
> Wrapped in sweet clothes, rings put upon his fingers,
> A most delicious banquet by his bed,
> And brave attendants near him when he wakes—
> Would not the beggar then forget himself?
> (Ind.1.36–41)

He appropriates to himself the role of a stage director, a playwright, even a god; he will "practice" on Sly to make him "forget himself." This lord is no Prospero, and his transformation of Sly is of the most broad and external kind, but it is significant that even at this early point Shakespeare conceives of transformation in terms of dream. His seeming metamorphosis will appear to Sly "even as a flatt'ring dream or worthless fancy" (l. 44). The lord, as one might expect, takes a contemptuous attitude toward dreams, which he equates not only with "worthless fancy" but with lunacy (l. 63). He is the instrument of Sly's transformation but he stands outside of it, secure in his knowledge of the real state of affairs.

The sybaritic components of his intended charade—"wanton pictures," "warm distillèd waters," "sweet wood," "music," "a costly suit" (ll. 47–60)—anticipate the ministrations of Titania to the ass-eared Bottom (*A Midsummer Night's Dream* 4.1) whom Puck "translated" in similar fashion. The "wanton pictures" also continue the covert imagery of metamorphosis which began with "beast" and "swine."

2 SERVINGMAN: Dost thou love pictures? We will fetch
thee straight
Adonis painted by a running brook
And Cytherea all in sedges hid,
Which seem to move and wanton with
her breath
Even as the waving sedges play with wind.
LORD: We'll show thee Io as she was a maid
And how she was beguilèd and surprised
As lively painted as the deed was done.
3 SERVINGMAN: Or Daphne roaming through a thorny
wood,
Scratching her legs that one shall swear
she bleeds,
And at that sight shall sad Apollo weep,
So workmanly the blood and tears are
drawn.

(Ind.2.49–60)

These Ovidian reminiscences are of course a form of sexual temptation, with emphasis on verisimilitude, leading to the crowning jest of the substitution sequence, when the young page impersonates Sly's supposedly love-sick lady. But Adonis, Io, and Daphne are all associated with transformation myths, which here stand in ironic contrast to the false metamorphosis of Sly. The lord and his attendants are having a private joke, which is all the more telling for its appositeness to the play's major themes. They flatter Sly by comparing him indirectly to such august personages as Jove and Apollo, whose beloveds have undergone a number of startling transformations. When the disguised page enters, as he does almost immediately, the ribald joke is complete.

"Dream" in this context becomes a kind of code word, a sign for the initial inversion which is the Induction's central trope. What the lord insists are "abject lowly dreams" (Ind.2.32) are the only truths Sly knows. But there is an element of verbal ambiguity present as well. "Persuade him," the lord instructs his servants, "that he hath been lunatic";

And when he says he is, say that he dreams,
For he is nothing but a mighty lord.

(Ind.1.64–65)

"Nothing," here as always in Shakespeare, is a word of great power. While the sentence means "He is nothing *except* a mighty lord," articulating the deception, it is also capable of meaning "He is nothing—*but at the same time* a mighty lord." This is the essential ambiguity of the dream state, in which illusion and role playing reach their apex. So likewise the lord will insist to Sly at the close of his Ovidian catalogue, "Thou art a lord and nothing but a lord" (Ind.2.61). His remarks have one meaning to the gulled and another to the initiate. He himself is not confused as to Sly's identity, nor are we. Since we observe the mechanics of alteration, we know that Sly's metamorphosis, unlike Bottom's, is not a metamorphosis at all. But for Sly the situation is radically different. When he speculates

> Or do I dream? Or have I dreamed till now?

he is weighing the same two possibilities occasioned by the lord's unconscious pun on "nothing."

In a sense he is "dreaming on both," for the answer to both of these questions is no. The whole matter of dream is a fiction contrived by the lord. But Sly, accepting the dream hypothesis, is at a loss to know which of the two contrary states—tinker into lord or lord into tinker—corresponds to the facts. Since he is (ostensibly) *inside* the dream, his evaluation of it can only be subjective. As we have seen, this quandary is resolved in the direction of humor when Sly wholeheartedly attempts to embrace the page-turned-lady. In the main plot of the play, however, the same ambiguity is turned to metaphor, and assumes a more far-reaching significance.

Petruchio's device for controlling the quick-tongued Kate is itself a species of metamorphosis; as one of the servants points out, "he kills her in her own humor" (4.1.169). The fiction he constructs is that of the shrewish husband, irascible and determined not to be pleased, totally unresponsive to fact and reason—a personality wholly inconsistent with the Petruchio who wooed her. He arrives for his wedding dressed in rags, curses at the priest, announces he will not attend the wedding feast, and abuses his servants without cause, reversing in the process all her expectations about his behavior and calling into question that which she has taken for reality. The final reversal comes as he leads her supperless into the bridal chamber, where a servant reports that he is

> Making a sermon of continency to her,
> And rails and swears and rates, that she, poor soul,
> Knows not which way to stand, to look, to speak,
> And sits as one new-risen from a dream.
>
> (4.1.171–75)

Kate has now been placed in the same ambiguous position as Sly found himself in the induction. The dream from which she seems to have risen is a figure of speech, but her condition of confusion is very like Sly's. Here again there is a manipulator and a manipulated; Petruchio practices on Kate as the lord had on Sly. Significantly, this stage of wonderment, this subjectivity of experience and suspension of ordinary assumptions, is the turning point in the transformation of the shrew.

We are very far, yet, from the healing and transforming sleep of Lear, and further from the marvelous sleeps of *The Tempest*. Kate comes no closer to dream than a brief simile invoked by a minor character. The image of the "one new-risen from a dream" remains on the level of language and does not enter the action. But the symbolic possibilities of the newly wakened state are adumbrated here, and adumbrated the more clearly for the parallelism of this image with Sly's condition. When Juliet awakens from her deathlike sleep, when Hero returns so surprisingly from the dead, there is about them, however briefly, the same glow of maturation as we find in the transformed Kate. We are presented with a fundamentally psychological insight: the suspension of certainties and the interchangeability of reality and illusion result in a heightened self-awareness.

The Taming of the Shrew is thus a significant early venture for Shakespeare in the multiple meanings and uses of dream. It contains the germ of the important idea of transformation—an idea which was to become central to *A Midsummer Night's Dream*. At the same time it experiments with the structural presentation of dream in a manner closely related to the play-within-a-play. Perhaps its most interesting single element, however, is a playful —though artistically polished—manipulation of the terms of reality and illusion seen through the image of dream. The potential utility of such a manipulation, only partially glimpsed here, is what changes dream from a device to a subject matter; from *A Midsummer Night's Dream* to *The Tempest* these beginnings made in *The Shrew* are implemented with increasing skill and power.

Patriarchy and Play in *The Taming of the Shrew*

Marianne L. Novy

Some of Shakespeare's recent critics have seen Petruchio's behavior in *The Taming of the Shrew* as an attempt to teach Kate to play, to draw her into his games. Kate's final attitude, they suggest, is less a passive submission than a playful cooperation. Important as this reading is for its insight into the tone and theatrical effectiveness of *The Taming of the Shrew*, it should not dismiss for us the play's treatment of the social order and in particular of patriarchy—the authority of fathers over their families, husbands over wives, and men in general over women. Games, however absorbing and delightful, have some relation to the world outside them; children reenact threatening experiences to gain a sense of greater control over them, and they try out roles that they may use in their adult life. Likewise, the games in *The Taming of the Shrew*, almost always initiated by Petruchio, may have some relation to the patriarchal traditions of the world of the *Shrew* and of its audience. Why this ambiguous coalescence between Petruchio the dominant husband and Petruchio the game-player, between a farce assuming patriarchy and a comedy about playing at patriarchy?

The themes of patriarchy and play both come to the fore in the induction, in which the penniless tinker Christopher Sly is transformed by trickery into a lord and prepared to watch a comedy. This scene introduces a world in which all identify themselves by their place in a social and familial hierarchy; it prepares us for a theatrically self-conscious performance in which those "places" are dramatic roles. As the "real" lord entertains us by showing that Sly can take a completely different place in the social order, the play begins to raise the question of how much that social order is a human construction

From *English Literary Renaissance* 9, no. 2 (Spring 1979).

whose validity is more like that of a game than that of divine or natural law. In the first scene of the inner play, the easy role change between Lucentio and Tranio, a servant clever enough to hide his precise degree of initiative from his master, repeats that question. But the focus of the play is not on the apparent changes in social class permitted by changes of clothes; it is on Kate's movement away from her original rebellion. Unlike the other two changes, this one superficially endorses the social order, but here too details suggest analogies between the social order and a game.

Analogies between games and such apparently serious institutions as law and war received their first detailed discussion in Johan Huizinga's *Homo Ludens*. One main characteristic he identified in play and in such institutions is the establishment of a separate sphere limited in time and space. Modern psychologists often describe the experience of play in terms of power: it involves the feeling of mastery, the sense of being a cause, the assimilation of reality to the ego. In a different context, these terms could apply to the official prerogatives of the head of the family in an hierarchical society; perhaps it is the power over a limited sphere (the play world or the household) that contributes most to this ambiguous coalescence between Petruchio's possible roles. The sociologists Peter L. Berger and Hansfried Kellner make a similar comparison explicit in their description of the modern nuclear family as a "macrosocially innocuous 'play area'": "It is here that the individual will seek power, intelligibility, and quite literally, a name—the apparent power to fashion a world, however Lilliputian, that will reflect his own being: a world that, seemingly having been shaped by himself and thus unlike those other worlds that insist on shaping him, is translucently intelligible to him (or so he thinks); a world in which, consequently, he is *somebody*—perhaps even, within its charmed circle, its lord and master" ("Marriage and the Construction of Reality," *Diogenes* 46 [Summer 1964].)

The comparison between play and household power is particularly relevant to *The Taming of the Shrew* because Petruchio and the other characters play games—separable units of play—in a literal sense. Roger Caillois enumerates four basic types of games; two of his categories, agon (competition) and mimicry (pretense) are clearly present (*Man, Play, and Games,* translated by Meyer Barash). In all of Petruchio's scenes with Kate until the last, ambiguous one, his words and actions involve some kind of pretense. For a period of time in each, Petruchio behaves according to "the fiction, the sentiment of 'as if'" which in mimicry takes the place of rules. In his first meeting with Kate and their only scene alone together, he invents an imaginary Kate and an imaginary society that values her: "Hearing thy mildness praised in every town, / Thy virtues spoke of, and thy beauty sounded"

(2.1.191–92). He is using language with regard not to its truth value but to her response. This use of language is appropriate to a game; as Caillois suggests, "Games generally attain their goal only when they stimulate an echo of complicity." As game player and as wooer, Petruchio needs her response.

What Kate does is to initiate another kind of game—the only game in the play that she begins—a competition of puns. In language markedly earthier than Petruchio's overtures, Kate introduces animal imagery and first brings out the sexual meanings in his retorts, even while verbally rejecting him.

> KATHERINA: Asses are made to bear and so are you.
> PETRUCHIO: Women are made to bear and so are you.
> KATHERINA: No such jade as you, if me you mean.
> (2.1.199–201)

Petruchio joins in this game with gusto. He seems undeterred—even encouraged—when she calls him a fool, and indeed there is often a hint of invitation in the lines where she makes the charge.

> KATHERINA: If I be waspish, best beware my sting.
> PETRUCHIO: My remedy is then to pluck it out.
> KATHERINA: Ay, if the fool could find it where it lies.
> (2.1.210–12)

After a few more rounds, he changes back to the original game—although with the variation that now his praise of her social merit is contrasted with her reputation.

> 'Twas told me you were rough and coy and sullen,
> And now I find report a very liar,
> For thou art pleasant, gamesome, passing courteous,
> But slow in speech, yet sweet as springtime flowers.
> (2.1.237–40)

Repeatedly Petruchio manipulates the language of social convention and roles for his own purpose—his relationship with Kate. The way he talks about society proves him independent of its actual judgments and ready to reverse its expectations drastically. The one word which describes both a social virtue and Kate's current behavior—gamesome—describes his attitude here as well. Caillois identifies in play a polarity between "frolicsome and impulsive exuberance" and "arbitrary, imperative, and purposely tedious conventions." We might see Kate's enjoyment of this battle as a kind of wild exuberance, but "gamesome" may also apply to the ability to perform in a highly conventional civilization that she will show later. Petruchio, by contrast, seems to be using the language of the higher pole in the spirit of the lower. "Go, fool" (2.1.251), replies Kate to his praise, and she again moves the conversation down to earth; but this time the wordplay very quickly comes out just where Petruchio wants it:

> PETRUCHIO: Am I not wise?
> KATHERINA: Yes, keep you warm.
> PETRUCHIO: Marry, so I mean, sweet Katherine, in thy bed.
> (2.1.259–60)

And when the others return, she is quiet as he gives the explanatory fiction that, like the end of the play, makes crucial the private mutuality between husband and wife: "If she and I be pleased, what's that to you? / 'Tis bargained twixt us twain, being alone, / That she shall still be curst in company" (2.1.296–98).

From now on, Petruchio's games will have the endorsement of the husband's rights over his wife. Yet, to the extent that Petruchio's power depends on a public belief in patriarchy for its legitimation, he behaves paradoxically when he violates the conventions of the social order. Earlier he created an imaginary ideal world; in the wedding scene his play has more of the turbulence characteristic of the game that Kate began earlier. He plays the role of the "symbolic fool, who seems to have originated somewhere outside society and its normal laws and duties" (William Willeford, *The Fool and His Scepter*). In a not unfamiliar anomaly, the man in a position of relative social power laughs at the conventions of the society that gives him that power, while the woman subordinated by her society worries about its judgment of her. As she repeats the charge of folly, her concern for public opinion becomes explicit in the face of his provocation.

> I told you, I, he was a frantic fool,
> Hiding his bitter jests in blunt behavior.
>
> Now must the world point at poor Katherine
> And say, "Lo, there is mad Petruchio's wife,
> If it would please him come and marry her."
> (3.2.12–13; 18–20)

Petruchio's sabotage of wedding ritual concludes when he takes Kate away from the banquet while playing the role of the defender who will, he says, "buckler thee against a million" (3.2.239). He insists:

> I will be master of what is mine own.
> She is my goods, my chattels; she is my house,
> My household stuff, my field, my barn,
> My horse, my ox, my ass, my anything.
>
> (3.2.229–32)

This speech again shows the coalescence of the role of player and patriarch, for the terms in which he declares ownership—the objects into which he transforms her—are extravagant enough to be a parody of patriarchal attitudes. The climactic phrase—"my anything"—declares the infinite malleability of identity within his world. Whether this hyperbole is play or domestic tyranny, his pretense of defending Kate from the attacks of the wedding guests is a more obvious invention. Like his earlier invention of a private bargain between Kate and himself, it seems intended ultimately to create such a bargain.

The suggestions of companionship in the play motif receive a challenge from the animal imagery here and elsewhere. In the title, "taming" identifies the hierarchy of husband over wife in marriage with the hierarchy of humanity over animals. Furthermore, several curious passages associate marriage with beasts of burden—usually the grotesquely described worn-out horse. For enough money, according to Grumio, Petruchio would marry "an old trot with ne'er a tooth in her head, though she have as many diseases as two and fifty horses" (1.2.78–80). Biondello enjoys enumerating the ailments of the horse Petruchio rides to his wedding, and Grumio makes a comic routine of the couple's falls from the horse on the trip back. These passages make comic emblems for an unattractive picture of marriage. The farcical tone, however, distances the threat. Since the passages are extravagant to the point of parody, the workhorse image becomes part of a larger game.

But other images of animals and many of the more explicit comparisons between animals and people are directly in the world of play—the aristocratic world of the hunt. In the induction, the lord's pride and concern for his hunting dogs remind us that domesticated animals attain a different status in the social order; they can benefit from human care and contribute to human enjoyment. Their position changes from an abstract subordination to an active and mutual (if unequal) relation. Play and mutuality may be goals of taming. In Saint-Exupéry's *The Little Prince*, an anthropomorphic fox uses taming as a metaphor for the establishment of a relationship. Petruchio's falcon-taming involves more hierarchy and coercion, but it also involves a wish for play and mutuality. As the means of Petruchio's taming move from denials of food and sleep to denials of the trappings of fashion, the farce that depends on the audience's withholding sympathy (and can therefore verge on brutality) modulates to a higher level of comedy. In the most important scene for the play theme in the *Shrew*, the medium is the even more sophisticated one of language.

Both clothing and language are important concerns in the other plots as well, and there too they can be material for play, but the effect is more obvious and more superficial. The lord makes a game of costuming Christopher Sly for his rise in the social hierarchy: Tranio's masquerade as his master Lucentio provides obvious enjoyment for the servant. When his former master Vincentio appears in Padua, Tranio refuses to recognize him, saying, "Why sir, what 'cerns it you if I wear pearl and gold? I thank my good father, I am able to maintain it" (5.1.73–75). Petruchio, by contrast, is not interested in using clothes as signs of a playful or serious rise in the social hierarchy. Instead, his choice of clothes for the roles he plays dramatizes his independence of the status concerns usually coded by Elizabethan clothing. Instead of dressing up for his wedding, he wears the most grotesque old clothes he can find—in their lumpish disproportion, he may be literally dressing like a fool. He pretends to offer Kate new clothes, as he pretends to offer her the food and sleep that are also conventional symbols of regeneration used parodically in the induction. His subsequent reversals have more function than frustrating her; like the fool's costume, they act out his scorn for convention and his preference for internal rather than external values.

> To me she's married, not unto my clothes.
> Could I repair what she will wear in me
> As I can change these poor accoutrements,
> 'Twere well for Kate and better for myself.
> (3.2.117–20)

> 'Tis the mind that makes the body rich,
> And as the sun breaks through the darkest clouds
> So honor peereth in the meanest habit.
> (4.3.171–73)

Kate, by contrast, is still concerned about fashion; she protests, "This doth fit the time, / And gentlewomen wear such caps as these" (4.3.69–70). When she accuses him, "Belike you mean to make a puppet of me" (4.3.103), he pretends to think she is talking to the tailor; and this pseudomisunderstanding raises the question of which rules are more restricting, Petruchio's or the anonymous judgments of fashion and other social conventions. Thus, although characters in all plots play games with clothing, Petruchio's games challenge rather than pay tribute to the social hierarchy.

Language, like clothing, is a medium for the games in both marriage plots. We have discussed its use in the pun battles and imaginative fictions of Kate's first scene with Petruchio; several later scenes explicitly turn on questions of translation, naming, and meaning. Disguised as a tutor, Lucentio uses the pretense of Latin translation to convey his identity and intentions to Bianca. She adapts to this mode of translation easily; equivocation comes naturally to her, and she uses the trick not only to disguise his intentions from the other suitors but also to keep Lucentio himself in doubt. Petruchio's games create a private language between him and Kate slowly but more effectively. Infuriated by his criticism of the new cap, she wants to use language to express her feelings regardless of his reactions:

> Your betters have endured me say my mind,
> And if you cannot, best you stop your ears.
> My tongue will tell the anger of my heart,
> Or else my heart, concealing it, will break,
> And rather than it shall I will be free
> Even to the uttermost, as I please, in words.
> (4.3.75–80)

Petruchio's game of pretending to misunderstand her—he responds to her outburst with "Why, thou sayst true. It is a paltry cap" (4.3.81)—shows her that self-expression unacknowledged by a hearer is not enough.

Up to this point, the games Petruchio has begun have been played more on Katherine than with her. Typically, they have been pretenses that the emotional situation she experiences is far different than she feels it is. On their way back to her father's house, he finally begins a language game that turns on redefining the external world, and perhaps this different focus for redefinition makes it possible for her to join in and begin creating a new world and a new society between the two of them. He claims that the moon is shining, not the sun, and refuses to continue the trip unless she agrees; she consents to his bargain.

> Forward, I pray, since we have come so far,
> And be it moon or sun or what you please.
> And if you please to call it a rush-candle,
> Henceforth I vow it shall be so for me.
> (4.5.12–15)

She replaces a language determined by the external world as she sees it alone with another determined by her relationship with Petruchio: "What you will have it named, even that it is, / And so it shall be so for Katherine" (4.5.21–22).

Here, with comic literalness, the play dramatizes the point Berger and Kellner make that "the reconstruction of the world in marriage occurs principally in the course of conversation. . . . The implicit problem of this conversation is how to match two individual definitions of reality."

Their use of language and their relationship are now becoming the kind of game that Petruchio has intended: "Thus the bowl should run / And not unluckily against the bias" (4.5.24–25). In spite of the ambiguity of this image, now Kate seems more like a partner in the game rather than an object used in it. She participates with wit and detachment, agreeing that "the moon changes even as your mind" (4.5.20).

In the background is the traditional association of the moon with the transforming imagination, and perhaps also a self-conscious parody of stage conventions of description. Since, as the mechanicals in *A Midsummer Night's Dream* knew, it was impossible literally to bring in moonshine, the Elizabethan audience depended on the dialogue for indications of whether a scene was set in day or night. They must have frequently watched a nighttime scene in literal sunlight and used their imagination. By accepting similar conventions, Kate is following Petruchio in defining their relationship as an enclosed sphere where imagination can recreate the universe. At first it seems that it will be only Petruchio's imagination, but the entry of a stranger—Vincentio—heightens the possibilities of the game.

Vincentio, as an old man, represents the class at the top of the social order within a patriarchal society, but when he is with Katherine and Petruchio his identity is temporarily within their power. Petruchio gives Kate her cue by transforming him into a sonneteer's dream of a lady: "Such war of white and red within her cheeks! / What stars do spangle heaven with such beauty / As those two eyes become that heavenly face?" (4.5.30–32). While her acceptance of Petruchio's renaming began as accommodation, here Kate shows her own creative imagination at work. She further confuses the patriarch by emphasizing the youth of the "lovely maid" and "her" role in the familial order which Kate's imagination is temporarily subverting: "Happy the parents of so fair a child! / Happier the man whom favorable stars / Allots thee for his lovely bedfellow!" (4.5.39–41). It is as if, in the new world of the game, ordinary social identities and inequalities are arbitrary and unimportant because other identities can so easily be assigned—anything can be its opposite. Categories of day and night, young and old, male and female, lose their strict boundaries. It is interesting that Petruchio, who so often refers to his father, in this scene alone swears by himself as "my mother's son" (4.5.6).

When Petruchio returns them to the ordinary world, where Vincentio is "a man, old, wrinkled, faded, withered" (4.5.43)—epithets perhaps in their own way a subversion of patriarchy on the youth-oriented comic stage—Kate triumphantly apologizes, with another inside joke: "Pardon, old father, my mistaking eyes / That have been so bedazzled with the sun / That everything I look on seemeth green" (4.5.45–47). Petruchio is leading the dialogue, but Kate clearly plays an active role in what he calls "our first merriment" (4.5.76). Faced with irrational demands, she has experienced the benefits of seeing them as part of a game and playing along. It will soon become apparent that her education in folly has taught her how to live with relative comfort in a patriarchal culture, and this coincidence implies a certain detachment about that culture's assumptions.

As part of the structural emphasis on patriarchy, *The Taming of the Shrew* concludes with three scenes in which characters ask pardon of father or husband. We have discussed the ambiguity of the tribute in the first; in the second, Lucentio's apology at the same time announces his marriage to Bianca and his own true identity and saves his father from jail. By the end of the scene, the two fathers, Vincentio and Baptista, are still grumbling at the deception and insubordination, but young love has found its way. In his bliss Lucentio hardly notices the discontent of his father and father-in-law after his ritual apology, and Katherine and Petruchio turn it into entertainment. Petruchio wins Kate over to a further independence of social convention by drawing a kiss from her on the street. Thus the tribute to patriarchy is ambiguous here too, and these precedents hint at a continued ambiguity in the end.

Fathers are clearly important in the *Shrew*. The word "father" appears fifty-four times—more often than in any other Shakespearean play except *King Lear* and *Henry VI, Part III*. Lucentio, Tranio, and Petruchio all introduce themselves as suitors with reference to their fathers and identify themselves by patronymic at other times in the play. But Tranio and Lucentio are eager to introduce a counterfeit Vincentio as the father who will legitimate the wedding, and throughout the play the younger characters' words about tradition, loyalty, and hierarchy in general, as well as patriarchy, are frequently in pursuit of their own ends. This is a familiar ploy in comic societies; Ann Whitefield's use of it in Shaw's *Man and Superman* receives a more explicit gloss. In the opening speech after the induction, Lucentio proclaims his gratitude to his father and his intent to study virtue and moral philosophy; his servant Tranio, who can bandy classical allusions with the best, advises him to follow his own pleasure and "study what you most affect" (1.1.40). In their next conversation the two are already plotting how to win Bianca. Following his advice to his master, Tranio too can use the rhetoric of loyalty to his own advantage. He provides the hint for Lucentio's idea of disguising himself as a schoolteacher and Tranio as Lucentio, and then accepts the role with great protestations of dutifulness: "I am content to be Lucentio / Because so well I love Lucentio" (1.1.216–17). Lucentio's peculiar mode of Latin translation exemplifies not only a purposeful use of tradition but also the predominance of patriarchal images on the microscopic level: the Ovidian passage ends "*Priami regia celsa senis*." When Lucentio translates the last two words "that we might beguile the old pantaloon" (3.1.36), *senis*, at least, is being translated literally. Bianca too can use the language of tradition for her own advantage to play up to Baptista and discomfit Katherine. Although we have seen her ability to do what she likes with Latin, she refuses Hortensio's analogous attempt to woo her by writing new words for the musical scale. Her reason? "Old fashions please me best" (3.1.78).

Thus profession of traditional values in the *Shrew* repeatedly turns out to be pretext, and it is against this background that we must see the last scene. At the wedding banquet, sexual wordplay like that in Katherine's first scene with Petruchio spices the dialogue, but each set of puns concludes with a reaffirmation of sexual and social roles. Meanwhile the imagery again turns to sport, much of it sport in which animals and human beings collaborate. Petruchio and Hortensio cheer on the duel of insults between their wives, crying "To her, Kate!" and "To her, widow!" (5.2.33–34). Bianca resentfully asks Petruchio, "Am I your bird? I mean to shift my bush" (5.2.46), and leaves the room. Tranio, after comparing himself to a "greyhound, / Which runs himself and catches his master" (5.2.52–53), leads the others in returning to the attack on Petruchio for reversed hierarchy in his marriage: " 'Tis thought your deer does hold you at a bay" (5.2.56). After his delight in playing a role at the top, Tranio has returned to his original adjustment to a lower place; he pleases his master by using words of hierarchy against others.

The wedding guests speak of their insults as jests and appropriately it is through a game that Katherine and Petruchio finally justify their marriage. Proposing a wager for the most obedient wife, Petruchio speaks like the sportsman proud of the creature he has trained, even as he protests her superiority: "Twenty crowns! / I'll venture so much of my hawk or hound, / But twenty times so much upon my wife" (5.2.71–73). When the other wives refuse to come when called, they are refusing to play; Bianca sends word "That she is busy" (5.2.81), and the widow says Hortensio has "some goodly jest in hand" (5.2.91). Katherine, as we know, has now learned to play her husband's games, and after appearing at his command she brings in the recalcitrant wives. At his word—"Off with that bauble!" (5.2.122)—her cap becomes a fool's toy. The other women are still scornful of folly, and their anticomic language undercuts their position on the comic stage.

WIDOW: Lord, let me never have a cause to sigh
Till I be brought to such a silly pass.
BIANCA: Fie, what a foolish—duty call you this?
LUCENTIO: I would your duty were as foolish too.
The wisdom of your duty, fair Bianca,
Hath cost me five hundred crowns since supper-time.
BIANCA: The more fool you for laying on my duty.
(5.2.123–29)

Bianca's scorn for folly has modulated into a scorn for duty, although she has earlier spoken of duty to appear self-righteous before her sister—"So well I know my duty to my elders" (2.1.7). As in her Latin translation, she uses the word to mean whatever she wants, but not something her husband can rely on.

When Petruchio gives Kate her cue for her final speech, the Widow is still objecting from a spoilsport position: "Come, come, you're mocking" (5.2.132). Kate, however, talks on—and on. It is, of course, the longest speech in the play, and should hold the onstage audience rapt. There is no need to hear Kate speaking ironically to consider the speech more as a performance than as an expression of sincere belief; against the background of many other incidents in the play, it should be clear that sincerity is seldom so much in question as social ability in the tribute to traditional values. With the flexibility of the comic hero, Kate has found a new and more tenable social role, and plays it with energy and aplomb. Instead of her earlier colloquial and often bitter language, she now speaks eloquently in a higher style and dwells on the language of patriarchy: the husband is "thy lord, thy king, thy governor" (5.2.138).

She has found a way of using language which reconciles her to her society. Following a long tradition of conventional wisdom about marriage, she sees woman's place in the home and man's in the outer world. Elizabeth Janeway has shown that this tradition serves a mythological function much more than it accurately defines social history (*Man's World, Woman's Place*); and it is surely not for its factual value that Kate gives her audience—onstage and off—this idealized picture of marriage. Rather, the speech serves as a reassurance to them that Kate will speak to them in their traditional language—not a language subject to scientific verification but one which serves as a common code reinforcing its society's beliefs about its members' spheres. Within her society's worldview, however, she elaborates on that language, giving, and thus assuming a need for, an explanation of her society's expectations of women. Her definition of marriage thus introduces other elements than hierarchy: the husband is

> one that cares for thee,
> And for thy maintenance commits his body
> To painful labor both by sea and land,
> To watch the night in storms, the day in cold,
> Whilst thou li'st warm at home, secure and safe;
> And craves no other tribute at thy hands
> But love, fair looks, and true obedience.
> (5.2.147–53)

She speaks of marriage as an affectionate contract—a relationship in which both partners have a role to play. Assuming men's greater physical strength (and no other inherent superiority), she contrasts the roles in an hierarchical way, but the roles also relate husbands and wives to each other in mutual need and interdependence.

Meanwhile, Kate preaches some of the virtues traditionally praised and fostered in women—peace, service, love, obedience, flexibility, and sense of one's own limitations—and reconciles them with self-assertion; she holds the center stage while preaching humility. Thus her speech, like the quite different apologies she and Lucentio make to Vincentio, has a tone of triumph. Her energetic resilience helps distance the threatening elements of compulsion in Petruchio's past behavior. When she concludes by offering to place her hand below her husband's foot in an hierarchical gesture of submission, his answer sounds less like an acceptance of tribute than praise for a successful performance in a game: "Why, there's a wench! Come on and kiss me, Kate" (5.2.180). Indeed, the series of games and game images that has led up to this speech makes it possible to see her improvisation very much as a game. How different is an ingenious creation of a culturally sanctioned role from an elaborate masquerade? Since socialization is a process of learning roles, a sharp distinction between play and social reality seems difficult to maintain even offstage, and here we are dealing with the conclusion of a game within a play within a game within a play. If hierarchical societies perpetuate their structures by the roles each new generation learns to play, Kate's performance is a dramatically heightened version of the kind of compromise that keeps such a society going and can at best afford its members a sense of enjoyment and creativity within strict limits.

Kate's new command of socially approved language corresponds to a new command of social convention; she is no longer ashamed to kiss her husband in public, and can still draw Vincentio's patriarchal approval: " 'Tis a good hearing when children are toward" (5.2.182). With social praise surrounding wife and husband for the order in their marriage, Petruchio is free to leave the banquet saying frankly, "Come, Kate, we'll to bed" (5.2.184).

Before he leaves, however, he sets up another hierarchy different from the marital hierarchy which has been the foundation of Kate's language: "We three are married, but you two are sped. / 'Twas I won the wager, though you hit the white, / And being a winner, God give you good night" (5.2.185–87). In most other Shakespearean comedies the final scenes are filled with reconciliations; here distinctions prevail, and these distinctions heighten the sense of privacy, of a separate, limited world, about the marriage of Kate and Petruchio. When Kate reprimands the other wives, she confirms her uniqueness as the only Shakespearean comic heroine without a female friend at any point in the play. For all the patriarchal approval, the character distribution gives her and Petruchio exclusive dependence on each other; it presents their marriage as a private world, a joke that the rest of the characters miss, a game that excludes all but the two of them.

Interestingly, architectural evidence suggests an increased sense of privacy about marriage in Shakespeare's time. From 1570 on, many English people rebuilt their houses to produce more rooms—most notably, a private bedroom for the married couple. Perhaps the spread of the ideal of privacy was related to changing beliefs about the relations between husband and wife among Shakespeare's contemporaries. Shakespeare shared his audience with Protestant preachers who were glorifying marriage much more than had their pre-Reformation predecessors. With their praise of marriage as spiritual companionship and their emphasis on the spiritualization of the household went an increased respect for the responsibility and personal virtues to be shown by women in marriage. According to Lawrence Stone, the puritan emphasis on the spiritual equality of women was probably also influencing the aristocracy; he points to the increased freedom that wills at this time gave daughters to refuse unwanted marriage partners, and he suggests that the larger number of separations and notorious quarrels among the peers between 1595 and 1620 might indicate that women were struggling for a better position in their marriages (*The Crisis of the Aristocracy 1558–1641*). Since divorce was illegal, and the power of traditional patriarchal ideology persisted, quarrels and separations would naturally result sooner than transformed marriage patterns. As William and Malleville Haller point out, patriarchal ideology also remains in the puritan preachers side by side with their new emphasis on companionship ("The Puritan Art of Love," *Huntington Library Quarterly* 5 [1941–42], 235–72). The popular preacher Henry Smith fills his *Preparative to Marriage*, published in 1591, with images suggestive of marriage as equal partnership. Husband and wife are like a pair of oars, a pair of gloves, and even David and Jonathan. He further notes, "Therefore one saith, that marriage doth signify merriage, because a plaifellow is come to make our age merrie, as Isaack and Rebeccah sported together." Yet a few pages later, he declares that "the ornament of a woman is silence; and therefore the Law was given to the man rather than to the woman, to shewe that he shoulde be the teacher, and shee the hearer."

Modern sociologists can, as we have seen, describe marriage as a play sphere with "mutuality of adjustment" and discuss the advantages for the husband of the role of lord and master without mentioning the disadvantages for his wife; similarly, *The Taming of the Shrew* combines patterns of patriarchy and companionship that members of its society may also have been combining. What is the role of play in this combination? Or, to rephrase an earlier question, what is the relationship between patriarchy *per se* and patriarchy as played by Petruchio?

To answer this question, we should first note that patriarchy itself rests on an ambiguity of values. The ideology of female subordination assumes the general superiority of men in physical strength; yet patriarchy also involves the subordination of the young to the old, and here physical strength yields to order, tradition, and experience. In dramatizing the relation of man to woman, the *Shrew* may assume patriarchy, but in dramatizing the relation of youth to age, it gives lip service to patriarchy and victory to youth—to Petruchio, who cuffs the priest at his wedding. But Petruchio's challenge to this aspect of patriarchy is not simply brute force: it is the energy of his words and imagination—his play—that verbally transforms old Vincentio into a young woman and back again with the utmost show of respect. Thus Petruchio's games combine the attractions of the rhetoric of order and the energy of disorder, while removing the dangers of both poles. Analogously, the game element in Katherine's characterization both removes the threat from her earlier aggression and adds vitality to her final defense of order.

In summary, the ambiguous combination of patriarchy and play in *The Taming of the Shrew* helps it appeal to spectators who are divided among and within themselves in their attitudes toward marriage. In a time of social transition when Renaissance England felt conflict not only between contrasting images of marriage but also between nostalgia for an older order and a new awareness of individuality, inner passions and outer chaos, the game element in the *Shrew* sets up a protected space where imagination permits the enjoyment of both energy and form, while the dangers of violence, tyranny, deadening submission, and resentment magically disappear. The game context permits Petruchio and Katherine to modulate from antagonists to cocreators of a new world to master and subject, and encourages the spectators to see as most important whichever pair of roles they choose and consider the others as "only a game."

Yet it may be significant that the mutuality between the main characters in Shakespeare's later romantic comedies never differentiates their roles to insist on the man as leader of the game. Indeed, in *Love's Labor's Lost*, perhaps written soon after *Taming of the Shrew*, Rosaline, the Princess, and the other ladies of France chastise Berowne, the King of Navarre, and their fellows for their assumption that as men they control the games; Berowne is to be purged by the frustrating task of jesting a year in a hospital. Perhaps Shakespeare sensed the costs of the differentiation of roles valued by a patriarchal society as he experimented with comedies in which the female characters took more initiative in games and in love.

"Kate of Kate Hall"

Ruth Nevo

A more gentlemanly age than our own was embarrassed by *The Shrew*. G. B. Shaw announced it "altogether disgusting to the modern sensibility." Sir Arthur Quiller-Couch of the New Shakespeare judged it

> primitive, somewhat brutal stuff and tiresome, if not positively offensive to any modern civilised man or modern woman, not an antiquary. . . . We do not and cannot, whether for better or worse, easily think of woman and her wedlock vow to obey quite in terms of a spaniel, a wife and a walnut tree—the more you whip 'em the better they be.

It will be noticed, however, that Q's access of gallantry causes him to overlook the fact that apart from the cuffings and beatings of saucy or clumsy *zanni* which is canonical in Italianate comedy, no one whips anyone in *The Taming of the Shrew*, violence being confined to Katherina who beats her sister Bianca and slaps Petruchio's face. Anne Barton has done much to restore a sense of proportion by quoting some of the punishments for termagant wives which really were practised in Shakespeare's day. Petruchio comes across, she says,

> far less as an aggressive male out to bully a refractory wife into total submission, than he does as a man who genuinely prizes Katherina, and, by exploiting an age-old and basic antagonism between the sexes, manoeuvres her into an understanding of his nature and also her own.

From *Comic Transformations in Shakespeare*. Methuen, 1980.

Ralph Berry reads the play rather as a Berneian exercise in the Games People Play, whereby Kate learns the rules of Petruchio's marriage game, which she plays hyperbolically and with ironic amusement. "This is a husband-wife team that has settled to its own satisfaction the rules of its games, and now preaches them unctuously to friends" (*Shakespeare's Comedies*). In our own day, the wheel, as is the way with wheels, has come full circle and the redoubtable feminist, Ms Germaine Greer, has found the relationship of Kate and Petruchio preferable to the subservient docility of that sexist projection, the goody-goody Bianca (*The Female Eunuch*).

With all this fighting of the good fight behind us, we may approach the play with the unencumbered enjoyment it invites. As Michael West has excellently argued, "criticism has generally misconstrued the issue of the play as women's rights, whereas what the audience delightedly responds to are sexual rites." Nothing is more stimulating to the imagination than the tension of sexual conflict and sexual anticipation. Verbal smashing and stripping, verbal teasing and provoking and seducing are as exciting to the witnessing audience as to the characters enacting these moves. It is easy to see why *The Shrew* has always been a stage success, and so far from this being a point to be apologized for it should be seen as exhibiting Shakespeare's early command of farce as the radical of comic action, a mastery temporarily lost as he struggled to absorb more rarefied material in *The Two Gentlemen* and only later recovered. The mode, however, of the sexual battle in *The Shrew* is devious and indirect and reflects a remarkably subtle psychology. Petruchio neither beats his Kate nor rapes her—two "primitive and brutal" methods of taming termagant wives, but neither is his unusual courtship of his refractory bride simply an exhibition of cock-of-the-walk male dominance to which in the end Katherina is forced to submit. Michael West's emphasis upon wooing dances and the folklore of sexual conquest is salutory, but Petruchio's conquest of Kate is far from merely a "kind of mating dance with appropriate struggling and biceps flexing." Nor is she simply "a healthy female animal who wants a male strong enough to protect her, deflower her, and sire vigorous offspring."

Only a very clever, very discerning man could bring off a psychodrama so instructive, liberating and therapeutic as Petruchio's, on a honeymoon as sexless (as well as dinnerless) as could well be imagined. Not by sex is sex conquered, nor for that matter by the withholding of sex, though the play's tension spans these poles. Christopher Sly, one recalls, is also constrained to forgo his creature comforts, a stoic *malgré lui,* and thereby a foil and foreshadower of the self-possessed Petruchio.

In the induction, the page Bartholomew plays his part as Lady Sly to such effect that Sly pauses only to determine whether to call the lovely lady "Al'ce madam, or Joan madam?" (Ind.2.110) or plain "madam wife" before demanding "Madam, undress you, and come now to bed" (Ind.2.117). Bartholomew must think fast, of course, and does: "[I] should yet absent me from your bed," he says, lest "[you] incur your former malady," and hopes that "this reason stands for my excuse" (Ind.2.124). Sly clearly has his own problems: "Ay, it stands so that I may hardly tarry so long. But I would be loath to fall into my dreams again. I will therefore tarry in despite of the flesh and the blood" (Ind.2.125–28). But Christopher Sly's "former malady" is, of course, an imposed delusion: it is not as an amnestic lord that he is himself but as drunken tinker. Katherina's, we will finally learn to perceive, was self-imposed, and requires the therapies of comedy—"which bars a thousand harms and lengthens life"—not the tumbling tricks of a "Christmas gambold" for its cure. This lower level functions as foil to the higher yardstick and guarantor of the latter's reality.

The play's formal *telos* is to supply that which is manifestly lacking: a husband for the wild, intractable and shrewish daughter of Baptista. But how shall Katherina herself not perceive that this husband is sought in order to enable her younger sister to be happily married to one of *her* numerous suitors? The situation of inflamed and inflammatory sibling rivalry which the good signor Baptista has allowed to develop between these daughters of his is suggested with deft economy. Her very first words:

> I pray you, sir, is it your will
> To make a stale of me amongst these mates?
> (1.1.57–58)

speak hurt indignity, an exacerbated pride. Her response when Baptista fondles and cossets the martyred Bianca:

> A pretty peat! it is best
> Put finger in the eye, and she knew why
> (1.1.78–79)

indicates her opinion that if Bianca is long suffering she is also extracting the maximum benefit and enjoyment from that state. Nothing that Baptista says or does but will be snatched up and interpreted disadvantageously by this irascible sensitivity:

> Why, and I trust I may go too, may I not?
> What, shall I be appointed hours, as though (belike)
> I knew not what to take and what to leave? Ha!
> (1.1.102–4)

These first glimpses already invite us to infer some reason for the bad-tempered, headstrong, domestic tyranny Kate exercises, but when we find her beating her cowering sister, screaming at her for confidences about which of her suitors she most fancies, and turning on her father with

> What, will you not suffer me? Nay, now I see
> She is your treasure, she must have a husband;
> I must dance barefoot on her wedding-day,
> And for your love to her lead apes in hell.
> Talk not to me, I will go sit and weep,
> Till I can find occasion of revenge
>
> (2.1.31–36)

we surely do not require inordinate discernment to understand what ails Katherina Minola. It is a marvellous touch that the pious Bianca, defending herself from the wildcat elder sister (with no suitor), says:

> Or what you will command me will I do
> So well I know my duty to my elders
>
> (2.1.6–7)

Bianca, it may be supposed, is not the only younger sister who has got her face scratched for a remark like that.

All of Padua, we are given to understand, is taken up with the problem of finding someone to take his devilish daughter off Baptista's hands, leaving the field free for the suitors of the heavenly Bianca. And this is precisely a trap in which Kate is caught. She has become nothing but an obstacle or a means to her sister's advancement. Even the husband they seek for her is in reality for the sister's sake, not hers. When she says: "I will never marry" it is surely because she believes no "real" husband of her own, who loves her for herself, whom she can trust, is possible. How indeed could it be otherwise since patently and manifestly no one does love her? Because (or therefore) she is not lovable. And the more unlovable she is the more she proves her point. Katherina of acts 1 and 2 is a masterly and familiar portrait. No one about her can do right in her eyes, so great is her envy and suspicion. No one can penetrate her defences, so great her need for assurance. So determined is she to make herself invulnerable that she makes herself insufferable, and finds in insufferability her one defence. This is a "knot of errors" of formidable proportions and will require no less than Petruchio's shock tactics for its undoing.

The undoing begins with the arrival of Petruchio, to wive it wealthily in Padua. No doubts are entertained in Padua about the benefits of marriage where money is, but it will be noted that no one is banking on a rich marriage to save him from the bankruptcy courts. All the suitors are wealthy; Lucentio, potentially at least. The contrast that Shakespeare sets up between Petruchio and Lucentio is an interesting ironic inversion of that obtaining in the Terentian tradition. In Terence the second (liaison) plot entailed tricky stratagems for acquiring money in order to buy (and keep) the slave girl. The main (marriage) plot on the other hand hinged upon the fortunate discovery of a true identity, which meant both legitimizing the affair and acquiring the dowry. Here, in the case of Bianca and Lucentio, the mercenary mechanics of matchmaking are masked by Petrarchan ardours on Lucentio's part (or Hortensio's, until the appearance of the widow):

> Be she as foul as was Florentius' love,
> As old as Sibyl, and as curst and shrowd
> As Socrates' Xantippe, or a worse
>
> I come to wive it wealthily in Padua;
> If wealthily, then happily in Padua
>
> (1.2.69–71; 75–76)

the spirited, bonny dark lass Baptista's terrible daughter turns out to be cannot but cause him a lift of the heart. She, for her part, does not of course respond immediately to his good-humoured teasing, but we may surely assume a certain vibration to be caused by this note of a tenderness which her obsessive fear of not finding has consistently put out of court. But she has built up sturdy bastions and will certainly not imitate her conciliatory sister. Combat is her chosen defence, and that these two are worthy opponents the set of wit which follows shows. Then comes the cut and thrust of the clash between her proud-mindedness and his peremptoriness. She misses no ploy, is outrageously provocative and brazenly impolite, verbally and even physically violent. He trips her up with a bawdy pun, she dares him to return a slapped face, and it is by no means certain to anyone that he will not. His strategy of mock denial:

> 'Twas told me you were rough and coy and sullen,
> And now I find report a very liar;
> For thou art pleasant, gamesome, passing courteous
>
> (2.1.243–45)

contains an infuriating sting in its tail:

> But slow in speech, yet sweet as spring-time flowers
>
> (2.1.246)

so that she is criticized for being what she most prides herself on not being, and consoled by being told she is what she most despises. Again:

> Why does the world report that Kate doth limp?
> O sland'rous world! Kate like the hazel-twig
> Is straight and slender, and as brown in hue
> As hazel nuts, and sweeter than the kernels.
> O, let me see thee walk. Thou dost not halt.
>
> (2.1.252–56)

And poor Kate must be beholden to him for patronizing defence against the alleged detractions of a despised world, and finds herself judiciously examined for faults much as if she were a thoroughbred mare at a fair. It is no wonder that in reply to his

> Father, 'tis thus: yourself and all the world,
> That talk'd of her, have talk'd amiss of her.
> If she be curst, it is for policy,
> For she's not froward, but modest as the dove;
> She is not hot, but temperate as the morn;
> For patience she will prove a second Grissel,
> And Roman Lucrece for her chastity;
> And to conclude, we have 'greed so well together
> That upon Sunday is the wedding-day
>
> (2.1.290–98)

she can only splutter "I'll see thee hanged on Sunday first"; a response which is immediately interpreted by Petruchio, for the benefit of the spectators, as a secret bargain between lovers:

> 'Tis bargain'd 'twixt us twain, being alone,
> That she shall still be curst in company.
> I tell you 'tis incredible to believe
> How much she loves me. O, the kindest Kate,
> She hung about my neck, and kiss on kiss
> She vied so fast, protesting oath on oath,
> That in a twink she won me to her love.
> O, you are novices! 'tis a world to see
> How tame, when men and women are alone,
> A meacock wretch can make the curstest shrew.
>
> (2.1.304–13)

Round one thus ends indeed with "we will be married a Sunday."

Sunday, however, brings not the marriage that has been prepared for in the Minola household, but a mummer's carnival. Petruchio arrives inordinately late, and in motley. Of the uproar he produces in the church we hear from Gremio, in a lively description containing the shape of things to come:

> Tut, she's a lamb, a dove, a fool to him!
> I'll tell you, Sir Lucentio: when the priest
> Should ask if Katherine should be his wife,
> "Ay, by gogs-wouns," quoth he, and swore so loud
> That all amaz'd the priest let fall the book,
> And as he stoop'd again to take it up,
> This mad-brain'd bridegroom took him such a cuff
> That down fell priest and book, and book and priest.
> "Now take them up," quoth he, "if any list."
>
> TRANIO: What said the wench when he rose again?
>
> GREMIO: Trembled and shook; for why, he stamp'd and swore
> As if the vicar meant to cozen him.
> But after many ceremonies done,
> He calls for wine. "A health!" quoth he, as if
> He had been aboard, carousing to his mates
> After a storm, quaff'd off the muscadel,
> And threw the sops all in the sexton's face.
>
> This done, he took the bride about the neck,
> And kiss'd her lips with such a clamorous smack
> That at the parting all the church did echo.
>
> (3.2.157–73; 177–79)

All of this is prologue to the first open clash of wills between these fiery newlyweds. He will instantly away, she "will not be gone till I please myself":

> The door is open, sir, there lies your way:
> You may be jogging whiles your boots are green.
>
> (3.2.210–11)

> Father, be quiet, he shall stay my leisure.
>
> Gentlemen, forward to the bridal dinner.
> I see a woman may be made a fool,
> If she had not a spirit to resist.
>
> (3.2.217; 219–21)

This is Petruchio's cue:

> They shall go forward, Kate, at thy command.
> Obey the bride, you that attend on her.
>
> But for my bonny Kate, she must with me.
> Nay, look not big, nor stamp, nor stare, nor fret,
> I will be master of what is mine own.
> She is my goods, my chattels, she is my house,
> My household stuff, my field, my barn,
> My horse, my ox, my ass, my any thing;
> And here she stands, touch her whoever dare,
> I'll bring mine action on the proudest he
> That stops my way in Padua. Grumio,
> Draw forth thy weapon, we are beset with thieves;
> Rescue thy mistress if thou be a man.
> Fear not, sweet wench, they shall not touch thee, Kate!
> I'll buckler thee against a million.
>
> (3.2.222–23; 227–39)

And he snatches her off, sublimely indifferent to anything she says, insisting upon his property rights, benignly protective, mind you, of his bonny Kate, turning all her protests to his own purposes and depriving her of any shred of self-justification by his indignant defence of her.

Stage-manager and chief actor, master of homeopathy—"He kills her in his own humour" as Peter says—Petruchio's play-acting, his comic therapy, provides the comic device. One of a long line of Shakespearean actor-protagonists, he holds the mirror up to nature, and shows scorn her own image. The tantrums that she has specialized in throwing he throws in superabundance, forcing her to see herself in the mirror he thus holds up.

Grumio's tale of the saga of the journey:

> Hadst thou not cross'd me, thou shouldst have heard how her horse fell, and she under her horse; thou shouldst have heard in how miry a place, how she was bemoil'd, how he left her with the horse upon her, how he beat me because her horse stumbled, how she waded through the dirt to pluck him off me; how he swore, how she pray'd that never pray'd before; how I cried, how the horses ran way, how her bridle was burst; how I lost my crupper, with many things of worthy memory, which now shall die in oblivion, and thou return unexperienc'd to thy grave.
>
> (4.1.72–84)

prepares for the continuing hubbub in the Petruchean dining-hall. That

Petruchio's strategy has the additional advantage of an austerity regime as far as food and sleep and "fine array" is concerned is all to the good. Petruchio is canny and will leave no stone unturned. Also, he has tamed hawks. But it is not physical hardship which will break Kate's spirit, nor does he wish it, any more than a spirited man would wish his horse or his hound spiritless. And Petruchio, we recall, wagers twenty times as much upon his wife as he would upon his hawk or his hound. Significantly, Kate's recurrent response to his carrying on is to fly to the defence of the cuffed and chivvied servants. Crossing her will, totally and consistently, under the guise of nothing but consideration for her desires, confuses and disorients her, as she complains to Grumio:

> What, did he marry me to famish me?
> Beggars that come unto my father's door
> Upon entreaty have a present alms,
> If not, elsewhere they meet with charity;
> But I, who never knew how to entreat,
> Nor never needed that I should entreat,
> Am starv'd for meat, giddy for lack of sleep,
> With oaths kept waking, and with brawling fed;
> And that which spites me more than all these wants,
> He does it under the name of perfect love;
>
> (4.3.3–12)

Katherine gets the point, but fails to get from Grumio even one of the mouth-watering items from a hearty English menu with which he tantalizes her. When she, listening hungrily to Petruchio's "sermon of continency," and knowing not "which way to stand, to look, to speak," is "as one new-risen from a dream," she might well rub her eyes, and say, with Christopher Sly, . . . "do I dream? Or have I dream'd till now?" (Ind.2.69).

What subtle Dr Petruchio has done is to drive a wedge into the steel plating of Kate's protective armour, so that he speaks at once to the self she has been and the self she would like to be; the self she has made of herself and the self she has hidden. The exchange of roles, with herself now at the receiving end of someone else's furies, takes her, as we say, out of herself; but she also perceives the method of his madnesses. Petruchio's remedy is an appeal to Kate's intelligence. These are not arbitrary brutalities, but the clearest of messages. And they are directed to her with undivided singleness of purpose.

In act 4 the remedy comes to fruition and Kate enunciates it:

> Then God be blest, it [is] the blessed sun,
> But sun it is not, when you say it is not;

> And the moon changes even as your mind.
> What you will have it nam'd, even that it is,
> And so it shall be so, for Katherine.
>
> (4.5.18–22)

And then it is enacted, with considerable verve, as she addresses Vincentio, on cue from Petruchio, as "young budding virgin, fair, and fresh, and sweet" and then promptly again, on cue, undoes all. Kate has yielded to a will stronger than her own and to an intelligence which has outmanoeuvred her, but the paradoxical, energizing and enlivening effect of the scene is that the laughter is directed not against her as butt or victim, but, through her prim performance, towards the disconcerted Vincentio. The *senex* is made fun of, in effect, by a pair of tricksters in some subtle alliance with each other not clear to him, but clear to the audience. Partly this response is structured by New Comedy paradigms. As Grumio puts it in act 1: "Here's no knavery! See, to beguile the old folks, how the young folks lay their heads together!" (1.2.138–39). But mainly I believe it is due to our sense of liberation from deadlock. Petruchio has enlisted Kate's will and wit on his side, not broken them, and it is the function of the final festive test to confirm and exhibit this. It is also to be noted that the arrival in Padua of Vincentio "exhausts" Lucentio's wooing devices, just as Petruchio's taming device exhausts its function; and it is a dexterous turn of composition which balances the mock non-recognition of Vincentio on the way to Padua, and his encounter with his Mantuan proxy, with the unmasking and recognition of the true Katherina, and the true Bianca, at the banquet.

That Kate is in love by act 5 is, I believe, what the play invites us to perceive. And indeed she may well be. The man she has married has humour and high spirits, intuition, patience, self-command and masterly intelligence; and there is more than merely a homily for Elizabethan wives in her famous speech:

> A woman mov'd is like a fountain troubled,
> Muddy, ill-seeming, thick, bereft of beauty,
> And while it is so, none so dry or thirsty
> Will deign to slip, or touch one drop of it.
> Thy husband is thy lord, thy life, thy keeper,
> Thy head, thy sovereign; one that cares for thee,
> And for thy maintenance; commits his body
> To painful labor, both by sea and land;
> To watch the night in storms, the day in cold,
> While thou li'st warm at home, secure and safe;

> And craves no other tribute at thy hands
> But love, fair looks, and true obedience—
> Too little payment for so great a debt.
> (5.2.142–54)

She wins her husband's wager but the speech bespeaks a generosity of spirit beyond the call of two hundred crowns. We have just heard Bianca snap at Lucentio mourning his lost bet: "The more fool you for laying on my duty," and it seems that the metamorphosis of folly into wisdom which the comic action performs makes an Erastian reversal. More fool the Paduans indeed, in their exploitative hypocrisies and meannesses, than this madcap pair.

The very un-Petrarchan Petruchio has been the initiator of remedies in *The Taming of the Shrew* as well as the temperamental suitor; Katherina largely a responder and a foil. These positions will be reversed in *As You Like It* but not without a number of intermediate moves. *The Two Gentlemen of Verona* which follows *The Shrew* allows very little scope for the presentation of independent action on the part of Julia (despite her notable independence) and no occasion for courtship at all. Nevertheless, the growth of perceptions which make later developments possible proceeds through this next play, and is positively advanced by its explorations in the ambivalent and mimetic rivalry of the gentlemen.

Coming of Age: Marriage and Manhood in *The Taming of the Shrew*

Coppélia Kahn

More than a difference of gender marks off Petruchio the tamer from Kate the shrew. He is a stereotype, animated like a puppet by the *idée fixe* of male dominance, while she is realistically and sympathetically portrayed as a woman trapped in the self-destructive role of shrew by the limited norms of behavior prescribed for men and women. Her form of violence is a desperate response to the prevailing system of female subjection; his represents the system itself, its basic mechanisms displayed in exaggerated form. The taming exaggerates ludicrously the reach and force of male dominance. Though it has long been recognized that Shakespeare gives Kate's shrewishness a psychological and moral validity lacking in all her literary predecessors, the corollary purpose of the taming as a farce has not been noticed. Unlike other misogynistic shrew literature, this play satirizes not woman herself in the person of the shrew, but the male urge to control woman.

Long before Petruchio enters, we are encouraged to doubt the validity of male supremacy. First of all, the transformation of Christopher Sly from drunken lout to noble lord, a transformation only temporary and skin-deep, suggests that Kate's switch from independence to subjection may also be deceptive and prepares us for the irony of the denouement. More pointedly, one of the most alluring perquisites of Sly's new identity is a wife whose obedience he can demand. As scene 1 of the induction begins, Sly suffers public humiliation at the hands of a woman when the Hostess throws him out of her alehouse for disorderly conduct. After he awakens from his sleep in the second scene, it is the tale of his supposed wife's beauty and Penelope-like devotion that

From *Man's Estate: Masculine Identity in Shakespeare.* University of California Press, 1981.

finally tips the balance, convincing him that he really is the aristocrat of the servants' descriptions. He then glories in demanding and getting his "wife's" obsequious obedience (Ind.2.68–75, 102–7). The humor lies in the fact that Sly's pretensions to authority and grandeur, which he claims only on the basis of sex, not merit, and indulges specifically with women, are contradicted in his real identity, in which he is a woman's inferior. Similarly, Petruchio later seems to find in Kate the reflection of his own superiority, while we know he is fooled by a role he has assumed.

In the main play, the realistic bourgeois ambiance in which Kate is placed leads us to question the definition of shrewishness the characters take for granted. In medieval mystery plays and Tudor interludes, shrews were already married to their pusillanimous husbands and were shown as domestic tyrants. Male fears of female freedom were projected onto the wife, who was truly a threatening figure because she treated her husband as he normally would have treated her. When the husband attempted rebellion, he usually lost. Shakespeare departs from this literary tradition in order to sketch Kate as a victim of the marriage market, making her "the first shrew to be given a father, to be shown as maid and bride" (Bradbrook, "Dramatic Role"). At her entrance, she is already, for her father's purpose, that piece of goods Petruchio declares her to be after the wedding. Baptista is determined not to marry the sought-after Bianca until he gets an offer for the unpopular Kate, not for the sake of conforming to the hierarchy of age as his opening words imply, but out of a merchant's desire to sell all the goods in his warehouse. His marketing technique is clever: make the sale of the less popular item the prerequisite of purchasing the desirable one. As Tranio sympathetically remarks after Kate's marriage is arranged, " 'Twas a commodity that lay fretting by you" (2.1.321).

That money, not his daughter's happiness, is Baptista's real concern in matchmaking becomes evident when Petruchio brusquely makes his bid for Kate. Both Petruchio and Baptista pretend to make Kate's love the ultimate condition of the marriage, but then Petruchio simply lies in asserting that she has fallen in love with him at first sight. Her father, though he doubts this farfetched claim ("I know not what to say") claps up the match anyhow, for on it depends Bianca's match as well. Both marriages, we can assume, provide insurance against having to support his daughters in widowhood, promise grandsons to whom he may pass on the management and possession of his property, and impart to his household the prestige of "marrying well," for the wealth of the grooms advertises Baptista's own financial status. Petruchio's and Tranio/Lucentio's frequent references to their respective fathers' wealth and reputations remind us that wealth and reputation pass from father to son, with woman as mere accessory to the passing. As Simone de Beauvoir states in *The Second Sex*,

> The interests of property require among nobility and bourgeoisie that a single administrator take charge. This could be a single woman; her abilities were admitted; but from feudal times to our days the married woman has been deliberately sacrificed to private property. The richer the husband, the greater the dependence of the wife; the more powerful he feels socially and economically, the more authoritatively he plays the *paterfamilias*.

Even the Bianca plot emphasizes heavily the venal aspects of marriage, though it is usually characterized as romantic, in contrast to the realism and farce of the taming. In act 2, scene 1, Baptista awards Bianca to Tranio/ Lucentio solely because he offers more cash and property as "widowhood" (that is, claims to have more total wealth) than Gremio does. As George Hibbard has shown, the scene satirizes the hardheaded commercial nature of marital arrangements.

It is time to turn, with Kate, from the father to the husband. From the moment Petruchio commands his servant "knock, I say," he evokes and creates noise and violence. A hubbub of loud speech, beatings, and quarrelsomeness surrounds him. "The swelling Adriatic seas" and "thunder when the clouds in autumn crack" are a familiar part of his experience, which he easily masters with his own force of will or physical strength. Like Adam, he is lord over nature, and his own violence has been well legitimized by society, unlike Kate's, which has marked her as unnatural and abhorrent. But let us examine the nature of Petruchio's violence compared to Kate's.

The hallmark of a shrew is her scolding tongue and loud raucous voice—a verbal violence befitting woman, since her limbs are traditionally weak. It is interesting that Kate is given only twelve lines in her entrance scene, only five of which allude to physical violence:

> I' faith, sir, you shall never need to fear;
> Iwis it [marriage] is not halfway to her heart.
> But if it were, doubt not her care should be
> To comb your noddle with a three-legged stool
> And paint your face and use you like a fool.
>
> (1.1.61–65)

Here she threatens Hortensio in response to his greater threat, that no man will marry her. These lines have a distinctly defensive cast; Kate refers to herself in the third person and denies any interest in a mate because two prospective mates (Hortensio and Gremio) have just made it clear that they have no interest in her. Kate's vision of breaking furniture over a husband's head is hypothetically couched in the subjunctive. Yet later Tranio describes her speech in this scene as "such a storm that mortal ears might hardly endure the din" (1.1.172–73). Throughout the play, this kind of disparity between the extent and nature of Kate's "shrewish" behavior and the male characters' perceptions of it focuses our attention on masculine behavior and attitudes that stereotype women as either submissive and desirable or rebellious and shrewish. Kate is called devil, hell, curst, shrewd (shrewish), and wildcat and referred to in other insulting ways because, powerless to change her situation, she *talks* about it. That her speech is defensive rather than offensive in origin, and psychologically necessary for her survival, is eloquently conveyed by her own lines:

> My tongue will tell the anger of my heart,
> Or else my heart, concealing it, will break,
> And rather than it shall I will be free
> Even to the uttermost, as I please, in words.
> (4.3.77–80)

Though she commits four acts of physical violence onstage (binding and striking Bianca, breaking a lute over Hortensio's head, hitting Petruchio and then Grumio), in each instance the dramatic context suggests that she strikes out because of provocation or intimidation resulting from her status as a woman. For example, the language in which her music lesson with Hortensio is described conveys the idea that it is but another masculine attempt to subjugate woman. "Why, then thou canst not break her to the lute?" asks Baptista. "I did but tell her she mistook her frets / And bowed her hand to teach her fingering," replies Hortensio (2.1.147, 149–50). Later Petruchio explicitly attempts to "break" Kate to his will, and throughout the play men tell her that she "mistakes her frets"—that her anger is unjustified.

On the other hand, Petruchio's confident references to "great ordnance in the field" and the "loud 'larums, neighing steeds, trumpets' clang" of battle bespeak a lifelong acquaintance with organized violence as a masculine vocation. The loud oaths with which he orders his servants about and startles the priest in the wedding service are thus farcical exaggerations of normal masculine behavior. In its volume and vigor, his speech also suggests a robust manliness that would make him attractive to the woman who desires a master (or who wants to identify with power in its most accessible form).

But if Petruchio were female, he would be known as a shrew and shunned accordingly by men. Behavior desirable in a male automatically prohibits similar behavior in a female, for woman must mold herself to be complementary to man, not competitive with him. When Petruchio declares, "I am as peremptory as she proud-minded," he seems to state that he and his bride-to-be are two of a kind. But that "kind," bold, independent, self-assertive, must only be male. Thus his image of himself and Kate as "two raging fires" ends on a predictable note:

> And where two raging fires meet together
> They do consume the thing that feeds their fury.
> Though little fire grows great with little wind,
> Yet extreme gusts will blow out fire and all.
> So I to her, *and so she yields to me*,
> For I am rough and woo not like a babe.
>
> (2.1.132–37; emphasis mine)

His force must necessarily triumph over Kate's because he is male and she is not. Those critics who maintain that his force is acceptable because it has only the limited, immediate purpose of making Kate reject an "unbecoming" mode of behavior miss the real point of the taming. The overt force Petruchio wields over Kate by marrying her against her will in the first place and then by denying her every wish and comfort, by stamping, shouting, reducing her to exhaustion, etc., is but a farcical representation of the psychological realities of marriage in Elizabethan England, in which the husband's will constantly, silently, and invisibly, through custom and conformity, suppressed the wife's.

In the wedding scene, when all the trappings are stripped away (and they are, by Petruchio's design), the groom is simply completing the legal arrangements whereby he acquires Kate as he would acquire a piece of property. Declaring he'll "seal the title with a lovely kiss," he refers not just to Kate's new title as his wife, but also to the title deed that, sealed with wax, passed to the purchaser in a property transaction. In the brutally plain statement Petruchio delivers at the conclusion of the wedding scene, he bears down on this point:

> She is my goods, my chattels; she is my house,
> My household stuff, my field, my barn,
> My horse, my ox, my ass, my anything.
>
> (3.2.230–32)

His role as property owner is the model for his role as husband; Kate, for him, is a thing. Or at least she will become a thing when he has wrenched unquestioning obedience from her, when she no longer has mind or will of her own. It is impossible that Shakespeare meant us to accept Petruchio's speech uncritically: it is the most shamelessly blunt statement of the relationship between men, women, and property to be found in the literature of this period. After the simple declarative statements of possession, quoted above, that deny humanity to Kate, the speech shifts to chivalric challenges of imaginary "thieves" who would snatch her away. Is she goods, in the following lines, or a medieval damsel?

> Touch her whoever dare,
> I'll bring mine action on the proudest he
> That stops my way in Padua, Grumio,
> Draw forth thy weapon, we are beset with thieves.
> Rescue thy mistress, if thou be a man.
>
> (3.2.233–37)

The point is that Petruchio wants to think of her in both kinds of terms. The speech concludes grandly with the metamorphosis of Petruchio into a knight-errant:

> Fear not, sweet wench; they shall not touch thee, Kate.
> I'll buckler thee against a million.
>
> (3.2.233–39)

The modulation of simple ownership into spurious chivalry reveals the speaker's buried awareness that he cheapens himself by being merely Kate's proprietor; he must transform the role into something nobler.

Petruchio's thundering oaths and physical brutality reach a crescendo at his country house in act 4, when he beats his servants, throws food and dishes on the floor, stomps, roars, and bullies. These actions are directed not against his bride but at his servants, again in the name of chivalry, out of a fastidious devotion to his bride's supposed comfort. But his stance is rooted realistically in his status as lord of a manor and master of a household that is not Kate's but his. He ordered her wedding clothes, chose their style and paid for them. Kate wears them not at her pleasure but at his, as Grumio's jest succinctly indicates:

> PETRUCHIO: Well, sir, in brief, the gown is not for me.
> GRUMIO: You are i' th' right, sir, 'tis for my mistress.
>
> (4.3.152–54)

In the famous soliloquy which opens "Thus have I politicly begun my reign" (4.1.182–205), Petruchio reduces Kate to an animal capable of learning only through deprivation of food and rest, devoid of all sensitivity save

the physical. The animal metaphor shocks us and I would sugges
to shock Shakespeare's audience, despite their respect for falcon
and that reverence for the great chain of being emphasized by E
Tillyard. The blandness of Petruchio's confidential tone, the swe
easy assumption that Kate is not merely an animal, but *his* animal, who lives or dies at his command, has a dramatic irony similar to that of his exit speech in the wedding scene. Both utterances unashamedly present the status of woman in marriage as degrading in the extreme, plainly declaring her a subhuman being who exists solely for the purposes of her husband. Yet both offer this vision of the wife as chattel or animal in a lordly, self-confident tone.

Shakespeare does not rest with showing that male supremacy in marriage denies woman's humanity. In the most brilliant comic scene of the play (4.5), he goes on to demonstrate how it defies reason. Petruchio demands that Kate agree that the sun is the moon in order to force a final showdown. Having exhausted and humiliated her to the limit of his invention, he now wants her to know that he would go to any extreme to get the obedience he craves. Shakespeare implies here that male supremacy is ultimately based on such absurdities, for it insists that whatever a man says is right because he is a man, even if he happens to be wrong.

Why does Kate submit to her husband's unreason? Or why does she *appear* to do so, and on what terms? On the most pragmatic level, she follows Hortensio's advice to "say as he says or we shall never go" only in order to achieve her immediate and most pressing needs: a bed, a dinner, some peace and quiet. Shakespeare never lets us think she believes it right, either morally or logically, to submit her judgment and the evidence of her senses to Petruchio's rule. In fact, the language of her capitulation makes it clear that she thinks him mad:

> Forward, I pray, since we have come so far,
> And be it moon or sun or what you please,
> *And if you please to call it a rush-candle,*
> Henceforth I vow it shall be so for me.
> . . . .
> But sun it is not when you say it is not,
> *And the moon changes even as your mind.*
>
> (4.5.12–15; 19–20; emphasis mine)

At this point, Hortensio concedes Petruchio's victory and applauds it; Petruchio henceforth behaves and speaks as though he has indeed tamed Kate. However, we must assume that since he previously donned the mask of the ardent lover, professing rapture at Kate's rudeness, he can see that she is doing the same thing here. At their first meeting he turned the tables on her, praising her for mildness and modesty after she gave insults and even injury. Now she pays him back, suddenly overturning his expectations and moreover mocking them at the same time. But he is not fooled and can take that mockery as the cue for compromise. It reassures him that she will give him obedience if that is what he must have, but it also warns him that she, in turn, must retain her intellectual freedom.

The scene then proceeds on this basis, each character accepting the other's assumed role. Kate responds to Petruchio's outrageous claim that the wrinkled Vincentio is a fair young maiden by pretending so wholeheartedly to accept it that we know she cannot be in earnest. She embroiders the fantasy in an exuberant declamatory style more appropriate to tragedy than comedy:

> Young budding virgin, fair and fresh and sweet,
> Whither away, or where is thy abode?
> Happy the parents of so fair a child!
> Happier the man whom favorable stars
> Allots thee for his lovely bedfellow!
>
> (4.5.36–41)

Her rhetoric expresses her realization that the power struggle she had entered into on Petruchio's terms is absurd. It also signals her emancipation from that struggle, in the terms she declared earlier: "I will be free / Even to the uttermost, as I please, in words."

Of course, a freedom that exists only in words is ultimately as limited as Petruchio's mastery. Though Kate is clever enough to use his verbal strategies against him, she is trapped in her own cleverness. Her only way of maintaining her inner freedom is by outwardly denying it, a psychologically perilous position. Furthermore, to hold that she maintains her freedom in words is to posit a distinction without a difference, for whether she remains spiritually independent of Petruchio or sincerely believes in his superiority, her outward behavior must be the same—that of the perfect Griselda, a model for all women. What complicates the situation even more is that Kate quite possibly has fallen in love with her tamer, whose vitality and bravado make him attractive, despite his professed aims. Her failure to pursue her rebellion after the wedding or in the country house supports this hypothesis, as does the tone of her mockery in act 4, scene 5, and thereafter, which is playful and joyous rather than bitter and angry as it was in the first three acts.

Finally, we must remember that Shakespearean comedy celebrates love; love through any contrivance of plot or character. Here Shakespeare parts company with sterner moralists like Jonson or more relentless social critics like Ibsen. As Northrop Frye states, "In comedy and in romance, the [illegible] seeks its own end instead of holding the mirror up to nature" (*A Natural Perspective*). Though Shakespeare quite astutely mirrors aspects of the human condition in this as in other comedies, that is not his only purpose/He also aims to present an idealized vision of love triumphant in marriage/The match between Kate and Petruchio bespeaks a comic renewal of society, the materialism and egotism of the old order transformed or at least softened by the ardor and mutual tolerance of the young lovers/Shakespeare wants to make us feel that Kate has not been bought or sold, but has given herself out of love./Thus he makes her walk a tightrope of affirming her husband's superiority through outward conformity while questioning it ironically through words.

In the last scene, Shakespeare finally allows Petruchio that lordship over Kate and superiority to other husbands for which he has striven so mightily. He just makes it clear to us, through the contextual irony of Kate's last speech, that his mastery is an illusion. As a contest between males in which woman is the prize, the closing scene is analogous to the entire play. It was partly Petruchio's desire to show his peers that he was more of a man than they which spurred him to take on the shrew in the first place. Gremio refers to him as a Hercules and compares the subduing of Kate to a "labor . . . more than Alcides' twelve" (1.2.256–57). Hortensio longs but fails to emulate his friend's supposed success in taming. Lucentio, winner in the other wooing contest, fails in the final test of marital authority. Petruchio stands alone in the last scene, the center of male admiration.

As critics have noted, the wager scene is punctuated by reversals: quiet Bianca talks back and shrewish Kate seems to become an obedient wife. In a further reversal, Kate steals the scene from her husband, who has held the stage throughout the play, and reveals that he has failed to tame her in the sense he set out to. He has gained her outward compliance in the form of a public display, while her spirit remains mischievously free. Though she pretends to speak earnestly on behalf of her own inferiority, she actually treats us to a pompous, wordy, holier-than-thou sermon that delicately mocks the sermons her husband has delivered to her and about her. It is significant that Kate's speech is both her longest utterance and the longest in the play. Previously, Petruchio dominated the play verbally, and his longest speech totaled twenty-four lines, while Kate's came to fifteen. Moreover, everything Kate said was a protest against her situation or those who put her in it, and as such was deemed unwomanly, or shrewish. Petruchio's impressive rhetoric, on the other hand, asserted his masculinity in the form of command over women and servants and of moral authority. Now Kate apes this verbal dominance and moralistic stance for satirical effect.

In content, the speech is thoroughly orthodox. Its sentiments, the platitudes of male dominance, can be found in a dozen treatises on marriage written in the sixteenth century. Its irony emanates primarily from the dramatic context. First, it follows upon and resembles Kate's rhetorical performance on the road back to Padua. It is a response to her husband's demand that she demonstrate her obedience before others, as she did then before Hortensio, and as such it exceeds expectations once more. It fairly shouts obedience, when a gentle murmur would suffice. Having heard her address Vincentio as "young, budding virgin," we know what she is up to in this instance. Second, though the speech pleads subordination, as a speech—a lengthy, ambitious verbal performance before an audience—it allows the speaker to dominate that audience. Though Kate purports to speak as a woman to women, she assumes the role of a preacher whose authority and wisdom are, in the terms of the play, thoroughly masculine. Third, the speech sets the seal on a complete reversal of character, a push-button change from rebel to conformist that is part of the mechanism of farce. Here as elsewhere in the play, farce has two purposes: it completes the fantasy of male dominance, but also mocks it as mere fantasy. Kate's quick transformation perfectly fulfills Petruchio's wishes, but is transparently false to human nature. Toward the end of her lecture, Kate hints that she is dissembling in the line: "That seeming to be most which we indeed least are." Though she seems to be the most vocal apologist for male dominance, she is indeed its ablest critic.

On one level, the denouement is the perfect climax of a masculine fantasy, for as Kate concludes she prepares to place her hand beneath her husband's foot, an emblem of wifely obedience. On a deeper level, as I have tried to show, her words speak louder than her actions and mock that fantasy. But on the deepest level, because the play depicts its heroine as outwardly compliant but inwardly independent, it represents possibly the most cherished male fantasy of all—that woman remain *un*tamed, even in her subjection. Does Petruchio know he has been taken? Quite probably, since he himself has played the game of saying-the-thing-which-is-not. Would he enjoy being married to a woman as dull and proper as the Kate who delivers that marriage sermon? From all indications, no. Then can we conclude that Petruchio no less than Kate knowingly plays a false role in this marriage, the role of victorious tamer and complacent master? I think we can, but what does this tell us about him and about men in general?

It is Kate's submission to him that makes Petruchio a man, finally and indisputably. This is the action toward which the whole plot drives, and if we consider its significance for Petruchio and his fellows, we realize that the myth of feminine weakness, which prescribes that women ought to or must inevitably submit to man's superior authority, masks a contrary myth: that only a woman has the power to authenticate a man, by acknowledging him *her* master. Petruchio's mind may change even as the moon, but what is important is that Kate confirm those changes; moreover, that she do so willingly and consciously. Such voluntary surrender is, paradoxically, part of the myth of female power, which assigns to woman the crucial responsibility for creating a mature and socially respectable man. In *The Taming of the Shrew*, Shakespeare reveals the dependency that underlies mastery, the strength behind submission. Truly, Petruchio is wedded to his Kate.

Horses and Hermaphrodites: Metamorphoses in *The Taming of the Shrew*

Jeanne Addison Roberts

The relationship between the world of nature and the world of human beings is always of special interest in Shakespeare's plays; and in discussing the "romantic" comedies critics since Northrop Frye have routinely noted the alternation in settings between the "normal world" and the "green world of romance" (*Anatomy of Criticism*). Just as routinely they have excluded *The Taming of the Shrew* from discussions of "romantic" comedy on the grounds of its "realism" and its farcical qualities (H. B. Charlton, *The Taming of the Shrew*). I should like to suggest that important elements of romance do in fact lie under the surface of this play and that an appreciation of these elements helps to illuminate its picture of the interaction of natural and human worlds. Some of the links between the worlds are supplied by Ovid.

I

It is a truth universally acknowledged that Shakespeare was well-versed in Ovid and that Ovidian literature shaped and permeated his writing. In the playwright's early works Ovid's influence is manifest especially in *Venus and Adonis* and *Titus Andronicus. The Taming of the Shrew* virtually advertises its Ovidian connections, with two Latin lines from Penelope's letter to Odysseus in *Heroides* actually quoted in Cambio's first Latin lesson with Bianca (2.1.28–29). There is a reference to *The Art to Love* (the *Ars Amatoria*) in the second Latin lesson (4.2.7). There are allusions in the play to the outcast Ovid and to Adonis and Cytherea, Daphne and Apollo, Io, Leda's daughter,

From *Shakespeare Quarterly* 34, no. 2 (Summer 1983).

Europa, Dido, Hercules, and the Cumaean sybil, all of whom Shakespeare could have learned about in the *Metamorphoses*. Even two dogs have Ovidian names: Echo and Troilus. And most suggestively for my purposes, there is, at the crucial moment of the play, a submerged but significant reminder of the myth of Salmacis and Hermaphroditus.

Superficially it might seem that the mythical and supernatural world of Ovid, with its obvious affinity for the gory surrealism of *Titus* and the rowdy eroticism of *Venus and Adonis*, would be antithetical to the realism and farce of *The Taming of the Shrew*. But I will argue that an appreciation of Ovidian overtones can move our perception of the comedy in the direction of romance, thereby enhancing our pleasure in the complexity of a play that is often thought to be lacking in subtlety.

Metamorphoses ought to be useful in comedy—a form committed by its very nature to the belief that people can change. Muriel Bradbrook has illustrated the use of metamorphoses in early Elizabethan dramas such as *The Old Wives' Tale, Love's Metamorphoses*, and *The Maid's Metamorphosis*. She observes, however, that the influence of such Ovidian transformations rapidly faded, and that Shakespeare never employed the device at all, since his comedies are concerned with the subtler forms of change involved in growing up (*The Growth and Structure of Elizabethan Comedy*). I think that Bradbrook is essentially right. Although there are hints of Ovidian metamorphoses in the transformations of Bottom and Falstaff, these metamorphoses pose a basic threat to comedy since the changes are nearly always for the worse.

Ovid's metamorphoses are, in fact, not true changes at all but terminal revelations of stasis. People turn into animals, trees, or stones because they cannot grow. Shakespeare's changes are more likely to be genuine. They are signaled by minimetamorphoses such as metaphors, pretenses, disguises, or stage images. They are distinctive in that they may be temporary or reversible, and they are often progressive rather than static or regressive.

Whereas in Ovid people turn into animals, a primary motif of *The Taming of the Shrew* is the elevation of animals into people—and not only into people but into suitable spouses, a rather more difficult feat. In the induction Sly is transformed from a monstrous swine-like beast (Ind.1.34) into a happy husband and a lord. And Kate and Petruchio move through a whole zoo of animal metaphors before they achieve the dignity of a human marriage. Each tries insistently and repeatedly to demote the other to bestial status. And while their refusal to respect the gap between animal and human in the Chain of Being is the stuff of low comedy, it is also a violation of humane interrelation. For Kate and Petruchio an important progressive image is that of the horse, and I shall pay particular attention to its uses throughout the play.

II

For the purposes of my discussion it will be helpful to abandon, at least for the moment, the received view of this play as a realistic farce controlled by the masterful Petruchio. It is true that the title invites this view and that folktales and analogues support it, but it is worthwhile to entertain the possibility of a subtext which runs counter to this traditional interpretation—a subtext resonant of romance and fairy tales in its depiction of two flawed lovers in quest of an ideal union. This approach flies in the face of long critical practice and requires a considerable suspension of disbelief, but it will, I believe, prove fruitful.

First, consider the "Induction." Why is it there? Why is it open-ended? Why does it linger repeatedly and, it seems, needlessly on details of sport and hunting? Why the persistent talk of dreams? Why the theme of deferred sexual consummation? And finally, why is Sly taken for his metamorphosis to the Lord's "fairest chamber" hung round with "wanton pictures," presumably those described later by the servants as representations of the metamorphoses of Adonis, Io, and Daphne?

The use of the induction or frame is, of course, a standard device of distancing, of signaling a movement from the "real" world to a domain of instincts, romance, and supernatural possibility. The classic instances are *The Thousand and One Nights* and *The Decameron*, but there are many other examples. The frame is not, however, a favorite Shakespearean device. The closest approaches to it in his other plays are the Theseus-Hippolyta plot in *A Midsummer Night's Dream* and the use of Gower in *Pericles*. In both cases the frame encloses a fluid romantic world within the fixed perimeters of known history. The repeated references to dreams in the induction of *Shrew* and Sly's resolve at the end to "Let the world slip" can be seen as creating a similar effect. The chief difference is that the frame in *The Taming of the Shrew* is open-ended.

Metaphors of the hunt and the use of hunting scenes serve regularly in Shakespeare as transitions between the worlds of history and romance, especially between the city and the forest. On one level this is predictable and obvious. Hunting is a sport that takes civilized man into the woods. But in myth and fairy tale the journey into the forest world is commonly an exploration of the instinctual and especially of the sexual. In *Shrew* the Lord moves from his offer to Sly of a "couch / Softer and sweeter than the lustful bed" of Semiramis (Ind.2.37–39) by natural progression to his offer of gorgeously trimmed horses, soaring hawks, and baying hounds. The servants switch easily back to images of lust—Venus's, Jupiter's, and Apollo's. These metaphors alert us to the important themes of animality and sexual pursuit in the play proper, and they ought also to sensitize us to the play's mythological overtones.

The fair chamber hung round with wanton pictures prepares, of course, for sexual themes. But even more important, it is a landmark on the road to romance. Frye points out that what he calls romances of descent frequently begin with scenes of passing through a mirror—as in the case of Lewis Carroll's Alice—or of sleep in a room with such modulations of mirrors as tapestries or pictures. Such sleep, says Frye, is typically followed by dreams of metamorphoses (*The Secular Scripture*). In the case of Sly, as in the case of the chief protagonists in *Shrew* proper, the metamorphoses we behold represent improvement, progress. Although Sly's transformation is superficial and externally imposed, we are not allowed to witness his regression. And the play convinces us that Kate and Petruchio are permanently altered. Only the merest trace of true Ovidian metamorphosis—the relevation of stasis—remains buried in the play. I hope to demonstrate this, as well as to show that the deferral of sexual consummation (made bearable for Sly by the diversion of the players) also energizes the courtship of Kate and Petruchio (premarital and postmarital)—not consummated, I suggest, until the latter's final invitation, "Come, Kate, we'll to bed."

III

As we turn from the induction to the play itself, the most obvious romance convention is that of the paired heroines. It is never safe, of course, to ignore the possible influence of available actors when one analyzes Shakespeare's practice in characterization; one remembers perforce the dark and blonde pairs of *A Midsummer Night's Dream*, and the double female roles of *The Comedy of Errors*, *Love's Labor's Lost* (redoubled), *The Merchant of Venice*, *The Merry Wives of Windsor*, *Much Ado about Nothing*, *As You Like It*, and *Twelfth Night*. But, although available actors may have facilitated its realization, the theme of the multiplication of lovers seems to have been central to Shakespeare's romantic comedy. Often such multiplication serves to emphasize the urgency and irrationality of sexual instincts. In *Shrew* it suggests rather the two sides of one psyche. One cannot make too much of the fact that Bianca and Katherina are sisters: the plot demands it. However, the dark, sometimes demonic older sister and the fair, milder younger sister *are* recurrent figures of romance (Frye cites the example of *Arcadia*), and frequently one sister is killed off or sacrificed in the renewal of the other's life. The argument for linking Bianca and Katherina can be made quite directly: the elder sister complains that she is being made a "stale" (one meaning of the word is "decoy," i.e., double) for the younger sister (1.1.58); Bianca's suitors hope to "set her free" by finding a husband for her sister (1.1.138); and the younger sister appears literally bound and enslaved to the elder at the start of act 2. When Katherina is carried away from her own marriage feast, her father placidly proposes to "let Bianca take her sister's room" (3.2.250).

Early in the play Katherina has been identified by everyone as an animal—not only seen as a shrew but also assaulted with an extraordinary thesaurus of bestial and diabolical terms. She is called devil, devil's dam, fiend, curst, foul, rough, wild cat, wasp, and hawk, to offer only a selection of epithets and adjectives. Bianca, by contrast, appears sweet, gentle, and compliant until two wry but telltale metaphors surface toward the end from the disappointed lovers, Tranio and Hortensio. The former remarks her "beastly" courting of Lucentio; the latter calls her a "proud disdainful haggard" (4.2.39). At the very moment that Kate is graduating to full human and marital status at the play's end, Bianca reveals her own animality with references to heads and butts, and heads and horns. Her words imply acceptance of animal status: "Am I your bird? I mean to change my bush" (5.2.46). At this point she says that, though "awaken'd," she means to "sleep again" (5.2.42–43); and she virtually vanishes, reappearing only as a shrewish echo in two final rebellious lines. The two figures have merged into one—one more fully human than either of the parts. This is the technique of folk tales rather than of realistic drama.

IV

The relationship of the two girls to their father is also of considerable interest. According to Bruno Bettelheim [in *The Uses of Enchantment*] children in fairy tales are turned into animals by parental anger. Baptista's favoritism toward his younger daughter is abundantly clear in the first scene: he assures her of his love; he praises her delight in music and poetry; and he singles her out for private conversation. Later (2.1.26) he angrily chides Kate as a "hilding of a devilish spirit" ("hilding" is a word applied to a horse in its earliest appearance in the *OED* in 1589); and, when a potential suitor for her appears, Baptista actually tries to discourage him. In fairy tales children transformed into animals are regularly turned back to humans by love, especially in marriage; but in addition they must establish harmonious relationships with the offending parent. It is significant, I think, that both Bianca and Kate are married in the presence of "false" fathers. Baptista never acknowledges a loving relationship with Kate until her transformation is revealed at the very end of the play; then he finally offers "Another dowry to another daughter, / For she is chang'd, as she had never been" (5.2.114–15). Bianca is married with the blessing of her own father (on the wrong man) and that of the Pedant, Lucentio's substitute father. The potential merging of these fathers into one true father is signaled on the road to Padua after the turning point between Kate and Petruchio when Kate says to Vincentio, Lucentio's true father, "Now I perceive thou art a reverend father." And Petruchio goes even further when he discovers the old man's identity, insisting "now by law as well as reverend age, / I may entitle thee my loving father" (2.5.48, 60–61). As daughters merge into one, so do fathers. In the last scene "jarring notes" are said finally to "agree," and Bianca and Lucentio welcome each other's true fathers (5.2.1–5). Lucentio has aptly summed up the situation with his declaration, "Love wrought these miracles" (5.1.124).

The forces working to metamorphose humans into animals are not merely parental, however. Katherina is associated with more animal metaphors than any other female character in Shakespeare. The images come from every direction, but especially from Petruchio. A great deal of the humor of the first meeting between Kate and her suitor (2.1.181–278), for example, depends on the determination of each to reduce the other to subhuman status. She connects him successively with a join'd-stool, a jade, a buzzard, a cock, and a crabapple. He responds by associating her with a turtledove, a wasp, and a hen—and of course his resolution to tame her implies the sustained hawking analogy underlying most of his behavior. In their first encounter each wishes to reduce the other to a laboring animal. Kate starts with "Asses are made to bear, and so are you," and the double (or perhaps triple) entendre of Petruchio's riposte, "Women are made to bear, and so are you," helps to activate a second animalistic analogy which underlies the play—the fallacious picture of beast and rider as a suitable emblem for harmonious marriage.

V

There can be no doubt that the equation of women with horses was operative in Elizabethan culture. Perhaps the most relevant example is that of one of the possible sources of Shakespeare's play, the long poem called "A Merry Jeste of a shrewde and curst Wyfe, Lapped in Morrelles Skin for Her Good behavyour" (London, 1580). The poem is of special interest because it too features two sisters (rather than the three sisters of the old play *The Taming of a Shrew* or the one sister of the source of the subplot, Gascoigne's *Supposes*), the younger and more docile of whom is cherished by the father and disappears early in the tale. In this poem the groom (the double meaning of this word invites equine elaboration) quarrels with his wife and in his anger mounts his old horse Morrell, a blind, lame nag unable to draw and given to falling in the mire; as he rides away, the groom conceives the idea of killing the horse, flaying it, and wrapping his wife in Morrell's skin "for her good behavior." There is no need to recount the brutal details of how he carries out his plan. The point is clear: he wants his wife to be a horse and, in effect, succeeds in turning her into one.

The association of women and horses surfaces also in other Shakespearean plays—notably in Cleopatra's envy of Antony's horse (1.2.21) and in Hermione's reference to women being ridden by their husbands (*The Winter's Tale* 1.2.94–96). In *The Taming of the Shrew* Gremio swears that he would give Kate's bridegroom "the best horse in Padua" and declares that in Petruchio's search for money he would wed "an old trot with ne'er a tooth in her head, though she have as many diseases as two and fifty horses." This grim marital metaphor materializes in the description of Petruchio's arrival at his wedding mounted on exactly such a horse; meanwhile, Petruchio himself has visibly deteriorated to match the horse. The play does not accept the emblem of horse and rider as a proper model for marriage. On the contrary, the Petruchio of this scene is, like his specifically characterized lackey, "a monster, a very monster in apparel, and not like a Christian" (3.2.69–70). Biondello says that it is not Petruchio who comes, but "his horse . . . with him on his back." Baptista's remonstrance that "That's all one" and Biondello's enigmatic and apparently gratuitous "A horse and a man / Is more than one / And yet not many" (3.2.84–86) might even be taken as a mock description of marriage—in which man and horse are one flesh. Petruchio has come, not like a proper bridegroom, but like a parody of the centaur at the wedding feast. However, he has none of the virility of the mythical centaur arrived to rape the bride. He looks readier for "The Battle of the Centaurs to be sung by an Athenian eunuch to the harp" than for sexual consummation. And though Shakespeare's play has nothing comparable to those lines in *A Shrew* that overtly reveal the bride's readiness for marriage, most stage productions supply some sign of her awakened interest in her suitor. Her disappointment in Petruchio's tardy and tawdry appearance reflects more than a concern about his breach of etiquette.

And yet the aura of the centaur is not altogether lacking. Petruchio does commit a sort of rape in carrying off his bride against her will. Nor is his comparison of Kate to Lucrece and Grissel unapt; he proceeds to treat her like each of these women in turn. There have been some overtones of the monster in Petruchio right from the start. Critics have often been conditioned by interpretations of the play that depict Petruchio as the wise teacher experienced in animal psychology, and by productions which encourage a blind enjoyment of his macho self-confidence. And yet the text does not necessarily support such responses. From the start Petruchio displays an irrational irascibility that leads his servant to call him mad and drives his friend Hortensio to rebuke him for the treatment he accords his "ancient, trusty, pleasant servant Grumio" (1.2.47). When the violent hero speaks of his coming to Padua as a way of thrusting himself "into this maze" (1.2.55) in order to wive, there may be some doubt as to whether he should be linked with Theseus or with the minotaur. As understandable as the expectation of a good dowry was to an Elizabethan audience, Petruchio's single-minded insistence that wealth is the burden of his wooing dance, and his willingness to accept a Xanthippe or worse if she is rich enough, seems the extreme of folly even to his friends. He compares himself and Kate to two raging fires which will consume "the thing that feeds their fury" (2.1.132–33). His thoughts of wooing are formulated with hunting analogies: "Have I not . . . heard lions roar? / Have I not heard the sea . . . / Rage like an angry boar chafed with sweat?" (1.2.200–202). And his courtship repeatedly reminds us of the hawking metaphor in which he sees himself as the hunter. Hunters in mythology, however, are often themselves in danger of metamorphosis, and from the moment of his venereal triumph Petruchio is transformed into a beast. Granted that his transformation is in part assumed, it nonetheless seems excessive and shocking. He is, says Baptista, "An eyesore at our solemn festival" (2.2.101), and his gross behavior in the church is carefully removed from view on stage. He is a "grumbling groom," "a devil, a devil, a very fiend" (3.2.155), and indeed Kate's journey with him to his country house is for her a descent into hell. The fairy tale of the two sisters is now eclipsed by shades of Pluto and Proserpina, or of Beauty and the Beast.

VI

The quester one finds in a fairy tale or romance is frequently accompanied by a dwarf or an animal. It is therefore both amusing and fitting to discover that Grumio, the first to speak in the new hellish setting of Petruchio's house, is a sort of dwarf, "a little pot" (4.1.5) and a "three-inch fool" (4.1.23), and that one of Petruchio's first acts is to call for his spaniel Troilus. Dogs, one recalls, are regularly resident in the lower world. Rather more significant is the description of the newlyweds' journey. In addition to the association of horses with women, it is a Renaissance commonplace that horses represent the passions, which must be reined in by the rational rider for a harmonious and moderate life. The skilled equestrian or the chariot driver . . . is a model for well-governed individual existence. The marital goal of Kate and Petruchio will be, not to ride each other but to ride side by side, in control of their horses, back to Padua. It is a goal constantly frustrated. The curious account of their problems with their horses en route to Petruchio's country estate has no parallel in *The Taming of a Shrew*. The idea might have been suggested by Morrell's tendency to fall in the mire or by a passage in Gascoigne's *The Supposes*, where Paquetto speaks of the "foule waye that we had since wee came from this *Padua*" and expresses his fear that the mule "would have lien fast in the mire." In Shakespeare the reported incidents (3.2.55–84) serve as fitting prologue to the scenes at Petruchio's house. Both Kate and her husband, it seems, have lost control of their passions (i.e., they have been thrown from their horses) as they came down a "foul hill." Kate's horse has actually fallen on her, and she has waded through dirt, "bemoiled" and disoriented. The suggestion that her former identity has been destroyed is supported by the discussion among the servants about whether or not she has a face of her own (3.2.99–104), and later by the report that she "knows not which way to stand, to look, to speak, / And sits as one new risen from a dream" (4.1.185–86). Unlike Proserpina, she is eager to eat in this frigid underworld but instead is starved (literally and figuratively), denied proper apparel (cf. Grissel), and assaulted with "sermons of continency" (4.1.182–83).

VII

Throughout act 4 Petruchio continues to speak of his wife as an animal, explicitly as a falcon (4.1.190–96), and to treat her accordingly. I have never found these scenes very funny. For me, they reinforce Curtis's observation that by now "he is more shrew than she" (4.1.85–86). Kate justly complains that her husband wants to make a puppet of her (4.3.103). The promised journey to her father's house is aborted by their quarrel over the time, and the horses to be ridden to Padua remain unmounted at Long-lane End (4.3.185). In act 1, scene 5 it appears likely that travel plans will be canceled again as the two start out for Padua a second time and momentarily disagree. But this disagreement leads to the turning point of their relationship. Kate learns to play Petruchio's game and acquiesces in his apparently whimsical identification of the sun as the moon.

It is at this moment that one encounters the submerged evocation of Ovid to which I referred earlier. Petruchio continues his game by addressing Vincentio as "gentle mistress." Hortensio protests that it "will make the man mad, to make the woman of him." But now the "game" turns suddenly into a kind of shared vision. Following Petruchio's lead, Kate greets Vincentio as "young budding virgin," and then goes on to say,

Happy the parents of so fair a child,
Happier the man whom favorable stars
Allots thee for his lovely bedfellow.
(4.5.39–41)

Editors have noted that this speech echoes Salmacis' words in Golding's translation of the *Metamorphoses:*

right happy is (I say)
Thy mother and thy sister too (if any be:) . . .
But far above all other, far more blisse than these is she
Whom thou for thy wife and bedfellow vouchsafest for to bee.

What has not been analyzed is the logic and significance of the connection. In Ovid Salmacis is addressing Hermaphroditus, the young man who subsequently fuses with her to become a hermaphrodite.

The language takes on obvious relevance in *The Taming of the Shrew*, where the speakers are transforming a man metaphorically into a woman. The word "bedfellow" evokes the idea of sexual consummation; and the hermaphrodite was a popular Elizabethan emblem for the miracle of marriage, which joined male and female. One emblem features, above the figure of the hermaphrodite, the sun and moon (on male and female sides respectively), reinforcing the idea of the union of these qualities in marriage and adding resonance to Shakespeare's scene, where the two heavenly bodies have become interchangeable. The alchemical Rebis features a similar image of the hermaphrodite flanked by sun and moon, symbolizing the first stage of the "chemical marriage" which produces pure gold. Another emblem shows the male and female being joined under a burst of light from heaven, comparable to the light that has "bedazzled" Kate's eyes. At this moment the hell of estrangement is lifted. Kate explains her vision as the result of "eyes, / That have been so bedazzled with the sun / That everything I look on seemeth green" (4.5.45–47). As a couple she and Petruchio have emerged from the underworld of lost and mistaken identities to the green world presided over by the true father (cf. *A Midsummer Night's Dream* and *As You Like It*). It is this moment that makes consummation possible. The same moment leads Hortensio to resolve to marry his widow and presumably coincides with the nuptial ceremony of Bianca and Lucentio. And following this moment, Kate and Petruchio mount their respective horses and ride to Padua.

Beryl Rowland suggests that the Latin word *equus* is related to the word for equal—because horses drawing a chariot needed to be well-matched (*Animals with Human Faces*). It is pleasant to suppose that some sense of this meaning inheres in Shakespeare's image, even though it is obvious that the idea cannot be pushed too far. There can be no question that the view of the dominant male and the submissive female survives to the end of the play. It would be absurd to argue otherwise. And yet the substitution of the vision of the hermaphrodite with its two human components for the earlier images of horse and rider or falcon and falconer is progress. And in independence of mind and liveliness of spirit the two riders do seem well matched.

VIII

In the final scene of the play bestial metaphors and figures of the hunt reappear—but with a difference. They are no longer in the mouths of Kate and Petruchio except when Kate rebukes the other women as "unable worms" (5.2.169). The widow's reference to the shrew is dismissed by Kate as a "very mean meaning" (5.2.31). Bianca speaks of head and butt, and head and horn, and "becomes" a bird to be hunted and shot at (5.2.46–51). Petruchio denigrates Tranio's greyhound imagery as "something currish" (5.2.54) and insists on the distinction between his wife and his hawk and hound (5.2.72–73). The transformation of the protagonists bodes "peace . . . and love, and quiet life." In this context the trial of Kate (a trial is a recurring feature of the final stage of romance) culminates in the revelation of her true identity and prepares the way for the long-deferred consummation.

The end of this play is not the social celebration characteristic of festive comedy. It shows, rather, the kind of individual salvation typical of romance. As Petruchio says, "We three are married, but you two are sped." The figurative transformation of Bianca into a bird is a true Ovidian metamorphosis—the revelation of terminal stasis. The lonely lovers create a private sanctuary for themselves, but the surrounding world continues to be paralyzed by its illusions.

The benign green world of *The Taming of the Shrew* is explicitly manifest only in the brief shared epiphany of the main protagonists. The violence, both psychic and physical, and the bestial metaphors belong to another kind of natural world—a world of nightmares and unrestrained instincts. The bestial metaphors are not merely weapons in the war of attempted manipulation of others; they are also passing pictures in a fluid scene where transformations are still possible. The very assertion of false images facilitates their confrontation and rejection. In the end it is possible to believe that Petruchio has given up his view of Kate as goods and chattels or as his horse or his falcon, even as Kate has relinquished her headstrong humor. It is, after all, the "sped"

Hortensio and Lucentio who persist in the assertion that Petruchio has succeeded in "taming" "a curst shrew." Petruchio himself is equally "tamed."

I am willing to concede that this is not the most obvious reading of the play. Still, if the romantic subtext I have attempted to trace is actually operative, it should not be totally ignored; and a stage production might effectively emphasize it. It demonstrates an oblique, probably unconscious, use of source materials which is, I believe, typical of Shakespeare. It also reveals the poet's uncanny ability to modify a standard tale of male supremacy with a humane vision which helps to account for the survival of his most sexist comedy as a play acceptable to and even pleasurable to modern audiences—truly a miraculous metamorphosis.

The Taming of the Shrew: The Bourgeoisie in Love

Carol F. Heffernan

Besides the much discussed romantic wooing of Bianca and rough taming of Kate in *The Taming of the Shrew*, there is a less noted but steady undercurrent of suggestion that calls attention to the fact that in the society of Padua marriage is a business and that, in general, this world is one where social position and wealth count for much. The play's concern with marrying well and with social status helps create the atmosphere of the bourgeois world of substantial citizens; *The Taming of the Shrew* shows Shakespeare's interest in the process of choosing mates in the middle class of his day. Comparison to the contemporary *The Taming of a Shrew* (possibly the source play), other related literary works, and manuals of domestic relations suggests that Shakespeare has purposely broadened the burgher aspects of the play to expose a real element of Elizabethan middle class life. There is much talk of contracts, dowries, property, clothes, and the things that money can buy. While Shakespeare does not ridicule bourgeois attitudes and values as Ben Jonson would, they are, nonetheless, one of the objects of his attention. Kate and Petruchio are shown to rise above them—at least, temporarily—and to a lesser degree so are Lucentio and Bianca.

Shakespeare fully establishes Petruchio and Lucentio, suitors for the hands of Baptista's daughters, as upper middle class citizens. There are indications of the wealth of their counterparts in *The Taming of a Shrew*, but Shakespeare in his play gives the matter of high middle class station more prominence than does the anonymous playwright of the parallel play. When in act 1 Lucentio first appears, newly arrived in Padua to begin his studies, Shakespeare has him talk about his background.

From *Essays in Literature* 12, no. 1 (Spring 1985).

> Pisa, renowned for grave citizens,
> Gave me my being and my father first,
> A merchant of great traffic through the world,
> Vincentio, come of the Bentivolii.
>
> (1.1.10–13)

Shakespeare makes clear that to be a merchant's son entailed considerable social and business responsibilities, for as Tranio points out, if Lucentio pretends to be a teacher in order to gain access to Bianca, many duties will go undone:

> who shall bear your part
> And be in Padua here Vincentio's son,
> Keep house, and ply his book, welcome his friends,
> Visit his countrymen and banquet them?
>
> (1.1.194–97)

Evidently Lucentio plays an important part in keeping his father's account books as well as in "public relations." That role is assumed by Tranio when he enters the intrigue for winning Bianca by pretending to be his master. When Tranio, as Lucentio, goes to seek permission of Baptista to woo Bianca, his "father's" merchant reputation serves him well, as may be seen in the following interchange:

> BAPTISTA: Lucentio is your name, of whence, I pray?
> TRANIO: Of Pisa, sir, son to Vincentio.
> BAPTISTA: A mighty man of Pisa; by report
> I know him well. You are very welcome, sir.
>
> (2.1.102–5)

Lucentio's actual merchant background stands in contrast to the pretended merchant identity of his counterpart, Aurelius, in *The Taming of a Shrew*. Ostensibly to test the sincerity of the love of Kate's sister (here, Philena, one of two), Aurelius sheds his princely status, gives it to his man, Valeria, and announces,

> when we come into hir fathers house,
> Tell him I am a Merchants sonne of *Cestus*,
> That comes for trafficke unto *Athens* heere,
> And heere sirha, I will change with you.
>
> (sc. 4, ll. 57–61)

But in the world of *A Shrew*, as in Shakespeare's play, to be a "merchant prince" is prince enough. Introduced as "a wealthie Merchants sonne of *Cestus*" (sc. 5, l. 165), Aurelius is welcomed by Philena's father, Alfonso (/ Baptista), who is himself a merchant: "Your welcom sir and if my house aforde / You anything that may content your mind, / I pray you sir make bold with me" (sc. 5, ll. 167–69).

Shakespeare is much more detailed about Petruchio's social position than the author of *A Shrew* is about Ferando's. Ferando has already arranged to woo Kate when *A Shrew* begins, so we have only an indirect report to start with, this the report of Polidor, a suitor for the hand of one of Kate's two younger sisters. Now knowing that Ferando has already arranged to court Kate, he puts him forth as one who by winning the older sister might free the younger ones to marry. He is clearly rich enough to be taken seriously: "he is a man of wealth sufficient / And for his person worth as good as she" (sc. 4, ll. 48–49). That's all we are told about Ferando's social position until Alfonso publicly announces his betrothal to Kate, "Give me thy hand, Ferando loves thee well, / And will with wealth and ease maintaine thy state. / Here Ferando, take her for thy wife" (sc. 5, ll. 43–45).

Shakespeare, on the other hand, directly reveals details about Petruchio's station in life and financial worth; he makes the audience a witness to Petruchio's acceptance as Kate's wooer and to his contracting arrangements with Baptista. First, like Bianca's main suitor, Lucentio, he gains admission to the house by establishing his pedigree: "Petruchio is my name, Antonio's son, / A man well known throughout all Italy" (2.1.68–69). And the almost formulaic invitation to court his daughter comes—"I know him well; You are welcome for his sake" (1.70). Furthermore, while the financial arrangements are struck between Petruchio and Baptista, we gain additional information about Kate's suitor. He is one of the landed gentry:

> PETRUCHIO: Signior Baptista, my business asketh haste,
> And every day I cannot come to woo.
> You knew my father well, and in him me,
> Left soly heir to all his lands and goods,
> Which I have bettered rather than decreas'd.
>
> (2.1.114–18)

There is something about the explicit obsessiveness with property and the fact of having "bettered" the land's worth through attention to "business" that suggests that Petruchio may be one of the *new* gentry. Petruchio's busyness hints at what Louis Wright describes as the "acquisitive habits of the middle class," which in Shakespeare's day "brought much aristocratic property into their possession" as well as titles of gentility (*Middle Class Culture in Elizabethan England*). Later in the same scene Kate's witty play with Petruchio over coats of armor may be seen as Shakespeare's glance at the controversy surrounding the right of the mercantile classes to claim coats of armor:

> PETRUCHIO: I swear I'll cuff you, if you strike again.
> KATHERINA: So may you lose your arms.
> If you strike me, you are no gentleman,
> And if no gentleman, why then no arms.
> PETRUCHIO: A herald, Kate?
>
> (2.1.220–24)

The very mention of arms in this punning passage suggests that Petruchio is one of the new landed gentry who has acquired something he would not wish to lose.

The actual courtships of Kate and Bianca reveal much about middle class domestic relations. Nevill Coghill is fairly representative of critical opinion in characterizing Petruchio as "a brute fortune-hunter." The characterization is Shakespeare's invention, though a glance at related literature on the shrew theme and at contemporary marriage manuals is enough to indicate that Shakespeare is merely exaggerating a type found in middle class Elizabethan life. Petruchio comes on the scene in act 1 a declared adventurer, out to find a rich wife:

> wealth is burthen of my wooing dance
>
> I come to wive it wealthily in Padua;
> If wealthily, then happily in Padua.
>
> (1.2.68; 75–76)

Even after Hortensio, one of Bianca's suitors, explains that Kate "is intolerable curst / And shrewd and froward" (1.2.89–90), Petruchio is determined to have her:

> thou know'st not gold's effect.
> Tell me her father's name, and 'tis enough;
> For I will board her, though she chide as loud
> As thunder when the clouds in autumn crack.
>
> (1.2.93–96)

And when Petruchio comes to settle the financial arrangements with Kate's father, Baptista, he comes right to the point: "Then tell me, if I get your daughter's love, / What dowry shall I have with her to wife?" (2.1.119–20). Baptista's answer being sufficient, Petruchio closes the deal with his offer that

> I'll assure her of
> Her widowhood, be it that she survive me,
> In all my lands and leases whatsoever.
> Let specialties be therefore drawn between us,
> That covenants may be kept on either hand.
> (2.1.123–27)

The cut-and-dried tone of these transactions bears out Maurice Ashley's observation that "most marriages among the landed gentry were unquestionably matter-of-fact property deals. . . . They were the result of hard bargaining, ending with the engrossing of deeds in a lawyer's office" (*The Stuarts in Love: With Some Reflections on Love and Marriage in the Sixteenth and Seventeenth Centuries*). Lucrative money arrangements were clearly a necessary prelude to Ferando's wooing Kate in *A Shrew*, though we do not witness the actual negotiations and they are, therefore, given less prominence. It is with obvious satisfaction that Ferando, on his way to court Kate, reports to his friend Polidor that her father "hath promised me six thousand crownes / If I can win her once to be my wife" (sc. 4, ll. 88–89). A similar note of monetary contentment is struck by the bridegroom on his wedding day in *A Merry Jest of a Shrewd and Curst Wife Lapped in Morel's Skin*, a ballad frequently mentioned in connection with both *The Shrew* and *A Shrew*: "Now shall I receyve an heape of golde, / Of pounds many one, and much goodys besyde."

Marriage handbooks, prized sources of advice on questions of domestic relationships, were found in many middle class Elizabethan libraries. Part of their appeal to the middle class citizen, no doubt, was the attention they gave to the problems of the family unit, the stability of which "made his goods safe and gave his accumulated possessions continuity" (Wright, *Middle Class Culture in Elizabethan England*). Among the matters addressed by these manuals is the question of arranging marriage contracts. In connection with Petruchio's dealings with Baptista it is interesting to note several representative comments which consider the arrangement of profitable marriage alliances. For example, the preacher Charles Gibbon, in a marriage manual titled *A Work Worth Reading* (1591), complains that in his day the aim of marriages is to match a rich man with a rich woman, whereas "The time was when rich men would have taken poore women to their wiues, and yet never made any respect of their portions, as Boaz did Ruth. He was a man of great authoritie and riches (Ruth 2.1) as some thinke iudge of Israel (Judg. 12.8), she a poore woman, that gleaned vpon his land for her liuing." That there was a need to make the point indicates how typical Petruchio's greedy motives were of the prospective middle class husbands of the time. Striking a similar note, Thomas Becon complains, "In these our dayes fewe mary in the feare and loue of god, while they all hunt and seke after mony, riches, welth. . . . If mony be present, nothing is absent." The greed of parents, eager to secure the most profitable marriage alliances for their children, was equally a target of the marriage manuals. In *Tell-Trothes New-Yeares Gift* (1593), a work of great interest so far as the family life of the middle class is concerned, Robin Goodfellow, just back from hell, relates to Tell-Troth the devil's boast that jealousy is one of the chief means of bringing people to his domain. There follows an account of the causes of jealousy and of unhappy marital relations, first of which is marriage for money:

> The first cause (quoth he) is a constrained love, when as parents do by compulsion coople two bodies, neither respecting the ioyning of their hartes, nor hauinge any care of the continuance of their wellfare, but more regardinge the linkinge of wealth and money together then of loue with honesty.

While Baptista negotiates with Petruchio without having consulted Kate, he does make a gesture towards making Kate's love the final condition of the marriage, for he tells Petruchio that the legal papers cannot be drawn up until "the special thing is well obtain'd, / That is, her love" (2.1.128–29). But Baptista is not truly interested in whether Kate's love has been won or not. When Petruchio lies, asserting that Kate has fallen in love with him at first sight, Baptista grabs at the match even though he doubts the unlikely claim—"I know not what to say" (2.1.318). Furthermore, Baptista actually doesn't seem too concerned with the financial details of Kate's marriage either. Relieved to have a reasonable suitor for the shrew, he doesn't haggle at all. Gremio, in fact, an elderly suitor for Bianca's hand who has witnessed the negotiations, observes, "Was ever match clapp'd up so suddenly?" (2.1.325).

Quite otherwise are Baptista's negotiations on behalf of his younger daughter, Bianca. Indeed, he signals that he has turned his attention to the marriage of his other daughter by referring to his altered stance. *Now* he will really get down to business. Comparing himself to a merchant venturer, he turns to Bianca's two suitors, old Gremio and Tranio (as Lucentio): "Faith, gentlemen, now I play a merchant's part / And venture madly on a desperate mart" (2.1.326–27). Baptista creates a contest of bidding between Tranio and Gremio by stating: " 'Tis deeds must win the prize, and he of both / That can assure my daughter greatest dower / Shall have Bianca's love" (2.1.342–44). Gremio enters into the competition by evoking the picture of a house, which Shakespeare must have intended as the quintessence of the new luxuries, new comforts, and new pleasures that the middle classes had come to enjoy in his day:

> First, as you know, my house within the city
> Is richly furnished with plate and gold,
> Basins and ewers to lave her dainty hands;
> My hangings all of Tyrian tapestry;
> In ivory coffers I have stuff'd my crowns;
> In cypress chests my arras counterpoints,
> Costly apparel, tents, and canopies,
> Fine linen, Turkey cushions boss'd with pearl,
> Valens of Venice gold in needle-work.
>
> (2.1.346–53)

The passage resembles the Marlovian catalogue found in *A Shrew* wherein the supposed father of a suitor for Kate's sister tries to impress the girl's father with his worth:

> If unto Cestus you do send your ships,
> Myselfe will fraught them with Arabian silkes,
> Rich affrick spices, Arras counterpoines,
> Muske, Cassiȧ, sweet smelling Ambergreece,
> Pearle, currol, christall, jilt, ivorie
> To gratulate the favors of my son.
>
> (sc. 16 ll. 12–18)

Both passages reflect a real burgher interest in living grandly and heighten the two plays' pictures of middle class milieus. The same aspect of contemporary taste is similarly captured in a prose work by William Harrison, *The Description of England* (1577): "Great provision of tapestrie, Turkie worke, pewter, brasse, fine linen, and thereto costlie cupboards of plate" filled the houses of "knights, gentlemen, merchantmen, and some other wealthie citizens."

Tranio more than matches Gremio's extravagant offers and to his triumphant advancement of an argosy—"What have I choked you with an argosy?" (2.1.378)—Tranio retorts with his winning bluff, "Gremio, 'tis known my father hath no less / Than three great argosies, besides two galliasses / And twelve tight galleys. These I will assure her" (2.1.377–79), adding to himself, "And twice as much what e'er thou off'rest next" (2.1.380). The extent to which Tranio has entered into the auction spirit Baptista initiated is best captured in the gambling language of his final comment on Gremio, "I have fac'd it with a card of ten" (2.1.405).

The business of vying for the beloved is a farcical underscoring of the crass materialism at the heart of middle class marriage arrangements. There is no scene of contending suitors in *A Shrew*; the episode is entirely Shakespeare's invention. Shakespeare may have found the seed of this scene, however, in a competition that appears in one of his sources for the underplot, George Gascoigne's *The Supposes*. In this play there is a competition between an old doctor, Cleander, and Erastrato for the hand of the heroine, Polinesta. Cleander needs constant reassurance from the parasite, Pasiphilo, that Polinesta's father will favor his suit: "whose welth? whose virtue? whose skill? or whose estimation can be compared to yours in this Citie?" He is, however, as unsuccessful as Gremio in Shakespeare's play. But Shakespeare makes the possibility of marriage to the *amans senex* very real. Baptista, convinced that Tranio can offer Bianca the most, settles on him, but not without stipulating that a binding legal contract be settled. Otherwise Bianca is to go "to Signior Gremio" (2.1.397). Thus Gremio is kept in reserve lest the "supposed Lucentio" not make good his bargain. Bianca could well be married to an old man without her consent.

A father like Baptista who stands ready to sell his daughter to the highest bidder illustrates the auctioneer tactics of parents who are criticized in Elizabethan marriage manuals. For example, we come upon the following passage in *The Passionate Morrice*, the sequel to *Tell-Trothes New-Yeares Gift*: "Fie, fie! marriages for the most part, are at this day so made, as looke how the butcher bies his cattle, so wil men sel their children. He that bids most, shal speed soonest." And we find Thomas Becon using the same cattle imagery in his *Boke of Matrymony*, Part two: "many parents at this day . . . do so handle their children as the Grasier doth his oxen and shepe, for as the one maketh sale of his beastes to such as wyl geue moste, so likewise do the othere of theyr children. Who offereth moste, he beareth awaye the ringe."

Since "old Gremio" is kept in reserve in case "supposed Lucentio" defaults on his generous offer, it is clear that Baptista gives no thought to the compatibility of the marriage partners. This compounds the callousness of selling Bianca to the highest bidder. Both arranging marriages for lucre's sake and indifference to matching the natures of the couple are subjects addressed in books of matrimonial conduct. Turning again to Thomas Becon's *Boke of Matrymony*, we find the following observation: "Too much wretched are those parentes, which enforce theyr children for lucres sake vnto suche maryages, as they from the verye hearte abhore." Charles Gibbon strikes a similar note [in *A Work Worth Reading*] when, in a debate between the characters, Philogus and Tychicus, he has the former say, against the argument that children cannot match without their parents' consent, "Alas, you doo not consider the innumerable inconveniences that bee incident to those parties which bee brought together more for lucre than loue, more for goods than good will, more by constraint than consent, nay more than that, you doe little way the inequalitee of yeares, the contrarietie of natures between age and youth."

Lucentio and Bianca are made to triumph over the commercial machinations surrounding the arrangements for Bianca's wedding. Baptista, having made the final financial negotiations with a man he supposes to be Vincentio, Lucentio's father, sends a messenger to Bianca to inform her that "Lucentio's father is arriv'd in Padua, / And how she's like to be Lucentio's wife" (4.4.65–66). But at the very moment the arranging of an assurance takes place between Baptista and the supposed Vincentio, the real Lucentio leaves to elope with Bianca before "the priest, clerk, and some sufficient honest witnesses" (4.4.94–95). Ready to evade ordinary bourgeois expectations, he says,

> 'Twere good methinks to steal our marriage,
> Which once perform'd, let all the world say no,
> I'll keep mine own, despite of all the world.
>
> (3.2.140–42)

And Lucentio is quite right. Even clandestine espousal, not a secret wedding ceremony, would have been binding, for as William Heale points out [in *An Apologie for Women*], if a woman proceeds to espouse herself without her father's consent, she is "vnhonestly espoused," but she is lawfully espoused just the same. Furthermore, had Bianca obeyed her father and married the "supposed Lucentio," two impediments would have stood in the way of a valid marriage which might have served later as grounds for annulment: "error of person (when the one you marry is not the one you thought him to be)" and "forced matrimoney." The elopement is unique to Shakespeare's play, though a minor rebellion against parental authority is found in *A Shrew.* There Aurelius, Lucentio's counterpart, marries below his station without his father's consent.

Kate and Petruchio rise above the middle-class commercialism of their marital arrangements even more dramatically, for the taming process, through which Petruchio gradually wins Kate's love and respect, involves flying in the face of middle-class formalities attaching to clothes, the decorum of weddings, and the rules of hospitality. Initially it appears that Petruchio looks forward to a substantial bourgeois wedding: "Sunday comes apace. / We will have rings and things, and fine array" (2.1.322–23). But he turns these expectations on their head. This is Biondello's description of Petruchio as he approaches—late—on his wedding day:

> Petruchio is coming in a new hat and an old
> jerkin; a pair of old breeches thrice turn'd;
> a pair of boots that have been candle-cases,
> one buckled, another lac'd; an old rusty sword
> ta'en out of the town armory, with a broken hilt.
> (3.2.43–47)

Even Petruchio's servant is badly set out—"a monster, a very monster in apparel, and not like a Christian footboy or a gentleman's lackey" (3.2.69–71). Baptista calls the clothes not merely inappropriate for the wedding day but a shame to his station:

> First were we sad, fearing you would not come,
> Now sadder, that you come so unprovided.
> Fie, doff this habit, shame to your estate,
> An eye-sore to our solemn festival!
> (3.2.100–104)

The matter of proper clothes is serious not only to Baptista but to Tranio who offers more proper attire: "See not your bride in these unreverent robes, / Go to my chamber, put on clothes of mine" (3.2.112–13). But Petruchio refuses and when Baptista complains about Petruchio's marrying Kate in such unseemly clothes, he speaks up for plainness:

> To me she's married; not unto my clothes.
> Could I repair what she will wear in me,
> As I can change these poor accouterments,
> 'Twere well for Kate, and better for myself.
> (3.2.117–20)

That Petruchio's behavior has not been a mere frolic is clear to Tranio who observes wisely that "He hath some meaning in his mad attire" (3.2.124). To be sure, the careless dress is part of Petruchio's scheme for taming the shrew, but it is also more than that. When Petruchio stands up for plainness, he reacts against the abuses of the class to which Baptista and Kate belong, and, in the particular instance of the church wedding, he appears to share the attitude of Myles Coverdale who [in *The Christian State of Matrimony*] complains that people attending wedding ceremonies enter the church "as it were into a house of marchaundise to lay forth their wares. . . . And even as they come to the church, so go they from the church again, light, nice, in shamefull pompe." Petruchio seems to have followed in part Coverdale's recommendation that the wedding be attended "without pomp . . . in . . . honest raiment, without pride."

The travesty of conventional behavior continues with Petruchio's wild manner during the ceremony. Gremio reports that the groom's swearing so shocked the priest that he dropped his prayerbook and that Petruchio "took him such a cuff" when he stooped to pick it up, that both it and the priest "down fell" (3.2.164). While tradition decreed that a cup of muscatel wine with cakes or sops were shared by the bride, groom, and company, Petruchio drank off the wine, threw the sops in the sexton's face, and kissed Kate with such "a clamorous smack" that Gremio left the church "for very shame" (3.2.178, 180). Finally, Petruchio, taking Kate, rudely leaves the ceremony without attending the reception, an especially rude breach of etiquette since earlier in the play, when he left Baptista to make preparations, he told him to arrange a grand affair:

> I will unto Venice
> To buy apparel 'gainst the wedding-day.
> Provide the feast, father, and bid the guests.
> (2.1.314–16)

Petruchio's failure to attend the reception is an abuse of bourgeois convention to which even a Puritan would be sensitive. William Gouge declared [in *Domestical Duties*] that the celebrating of marriages with feasting and merrymaking is in the nature of a civil ceremony and "very requisite":

> Though vpon the forenamed consecrating of mariage it bee in regard to the substance thereof fully consummate, yet for the greater solemnity of so honourable a thing, it is very requisite that further there be added a ciuill celebration of it: vnder which I comprise all those lawfull customes that are vsed for the setting forth of the outward solemnitie thereof, as meeting friends, accompanying the Bridegroome and Bride both to and from the Church, putting on best apparell, feasting, with other tokens of reioycing.

Clearly Petruchio's flaunting of conventional behavior is not indicative of a permanent rebellion against the values of his class. Gremio's questions to Curtis on arriving at Petruchio's country estate give some notion of the style in which life ordinarily proceeds there, particularly on festive occasions: "Where's the cook? Is supper ready, the house trimm'd, rushes strew'd, cobwebs swept, the servingmen in their new fustian, [their] white stockings, and every officer his wedding garment on? Be the jacks fair within, the Gills fair without, the carpets laid, and every thing in order?" (4.1.45–51). And

Petruchio's own words to Kate, as she hungrily eats the meat finally given her after being virtually starved, suggest that he retains a clear sense of what his class's standard is:

> Kate, eat apace. And now, my honey love,
> We will return to thy father's house,
> And revel it bravely as the best,
> With silken coats and caps and golden rings,
> With ruffs and cuffs, and fardingales, and things.
>
> (4.3.52–56)

But while the taming proceeds, these dainties are dangled only to be snatched away. When a haberdasher and tailor come on the scene offering caps and elegant gowns, Petruchio finds fault with their wares and, to Kate's chagrin, sends them on their way. Settling on the virtue of plainness as he did in the church scene, Petruchio declares,

> we will unto your father's
> Even in these honest mean habiliments;
> Our purses shall be proud, our garments poor,
> For 'tis the mind that makes the body rich.
>
> (4.3.169–72)

Ferando's words at this point in the action in *A Shrew* represent one of the few verbal echoes in the play:

> Come Kate, wee now will go see thy fathers house
> Even in these honest means abilliments,
> Our purses shal be rich, our garments plaine.
>
> (sc. 13, ll. 53–55)

Otherwise the taming scenes in *A Shrew* contain just the bare outlines of Shakespeare's plot. Ferando comes ill attired to church, but less is made of it and there is no description of his behavior during the wedding ceremony. The hasty retreat from the reception is handled more briefly as is the arrival at Ferando's country house and the scene with the tailor.

It is fitting that Petruchio's taming includes as one of its central elements an attack on certain middle-class values and conventions, for as Muriel Bradbrook has stated, "money helps to set the shrew where she belongs, within the merchant class." Nonetheless, Petruchio remains essentially a man of his class, however sincere his standing up for plainness may sound. In this he is perhaps akin to more virulent social critics, satirists like Shakespeare's Thersites and Ben Jonson's Macilente who, while attacking vice, contain within themselves many of the faults they censure in others. Though it might seem that social criticism would be more effective if the character who delivers it is the moral opposite of what he condemns, the fact is that the satirical tradition is full of "superior," yet defective critics. I do not mean to argue, however, that Petruchio is a satirist, but merely that some confusion may attend the fact that his is a critical voice arising out of a nature which contains contradictions. Marrying well, for example, remains a value he does not give up. Note his announcement to the real Vincentio, met on the return trip to Padua:

> Thy son by this hath married. Wonder not,
> Nor be grieved; she is of good esteem,
> Her dowry wealthy, and of worthy birth;
> Beside, so qualified as may beseem
> The spouse of any noble gentlemen.
>
> (4.5.63–67)

The arranged marriage may have been evaded, but the romantic one is as lucrative and brings with it a woman of as high station as any calculating arrangement might. Indeed, Petruchio closes the play as he entered it, joining love and money. He has won the wager: Kate comes obediently at his call while the wives of Hortensio and Lucentio sit talking. Besides, Baptista has given him twenty thousand crowns, "Another dowry to another daughter" (5.2.114) to honor Kate's new personality. With reason Petruchio can say boldly in an aside to Lucentio: " 'Twas I won the wager, though you won the white, / And being a winner, God give you good night!" (5.2.186–87). One implication of the play is certainly that life in this opulent world of Padua will go on in much the same way as before. But the abuses that Shakespeare exposes in this examination of bourgeois marriage patterns and social values have not been resolved, and are too serious to be dispersed in laughter.

Charisma, Coercion, and Comic Form in *The Taming of the Shrew*

Richard A. Burt

Modern critics tend to view Shakespearean comedy either as a celebration of social harmony or as an ironic, quiet subversion of that harmony. Critical disagreement typically focuses on the resolutions of the comedies: critics who see a restored and renewed community point to the marriages, banquets, and festivity of the endings, while critics who view the resolutions as ironic commentary argue that the presence of the Shylock, Don John, Malvolio, or Jacques is often disruptive of social harmony; irony is measured by what certain critics take to be a gap between the social harmony presumed by the characters and Shakespeare's sense that this harmony is achieved provisionally and at great cost. Despite this disagreement, all of these critics share a central assumption about the social function of the comedies: the purpose of the comedies is to resolve social conflicts conclusively, though for ironic critics they may fail to do so. I want to suggest that the comedies have a different social function. Community is formed and affirmed not by putting an end to social conflicts, but by managing and controlling them so that social norms are continually reinforced. This function is disclosed by the form of Shakespeare's endings.

Although critics tend to believe that the comedies have formal unity, they have been troubled by Shakespeare's dramatic closure because it violates formal unity in the most spectacular manner: closure is generally extremely artificial and arbitrary, often straining the bounds of credibility. Northrop Frye argues, for example, that "the drive towards a comic conclusion is so powerful that it breaks all the chains of probability in the plot, in habit and

---

From *Criticism: A Quarterly for Literature and the Arts* 26, no. 4 (Fall 1984).

in the characters, even of expectation in the audience" (*A Natural Perspective*). Similarly, Louis Adrian Montrose argues that to view "the happy endings of Shakespeare's romantic comedies as symbolic assimilations of potential disorder by a normative system" is inadequate because "Shakespeare's romantic comedies conclude on the threshold of marriage and parenthood. They end without the consummations and procreation which guarantee the continuity of the socioeconomic order; and without the comic society's assimilation of the incongruous perspectives opened up during the younger generation's marginal experiences in forest, darkness, dream, spell, disguise, and courtship game." The comedies do not fully incorporate "the challenges to the social order and orthodoxy" they present. René Girard argues explicitly that the endings are arbitrary (" 'To Entrap the Wisest': A Reading of *The Merchant of Venice*," in *Literature and Society*, edited by Edward Said). I will argue, however, that dramatic closure is in fact motivated by the social purpose of the comedies: the lack of formal unity and coherence critics have correctly perceived registers the ideological function of the comedies, namely, to coerce solutions to what are in fact unresolvable conflicts in the family and in the social structure of Renaissance England.

I want to advance my case by focusing on *The Taming of the Shrew* because critics have taken its formal problems to be entirely separate from the question of whether social unity is attained. The formal problem is twofold: not only does the Christopher Sly frame fail to return but the final scene itself is not required by the demands of the plot: a resolution has apparently already been achieved; both couples have married when it begins. It will be my contention, however, that the question of formal coherence is not in fact separate from the question of social harmony; indeed, the comic form of *The Taming of the Shrew* is shaped by its social function. Shakespeare's comedy does not resolve conflicts by putting an end to violence and aggression but controls conflicts through less obvious and more enduring forms of domination—discipline and coercion. Dramatic closure that is balanced, conclusive, and coherent does not occur precisely because social conflicts are never fully resolved: social harmony is possible only because Petruchio and Kate are differentiated competitively from the other couples through a wager. The fact that *The Taming of the Shrew* lacks formal coherence does not mean, however, that it should be dismissed as a crude, early comedy. I will argue, rather, that *The Taming of the Shrew* is paradigmatic of Shakespearean comedy: the fact that the social harmony achieved in the resolutions, inconclusive though it may be, is all that can be achieved, necessitates the sacrifice of complete dramatic closure.

The relation between the disappearance of the frame and the resolution of social conflicts within the narrative structure will become clear if we see that Petruchio's taming process is deeply in the service of patriarchy. There is currently a consensus among most critics that *The Taming of the Shrew* is a feminist critique of patriarchal views of women. In this account, Petruchio socializes Kate without depending on coercion or violence; instead Petruchio plays at patriarchy with Kate. If the threat of violence is present at all, it is only part of a temporary strategy Petruchio abandons as soon as Kate is tamed. What Petruchio wants, according to these critics, is not a traditional patriarchal relationship in which the husband rules the wife, but a loving relationship between equal and independent partners. Marianne Novy argues, for example, that "the game element . . . sets up a protected space where imagination permits the enjoyment of both energy and form, while the dangers of violence, tyranny, deadening submission, and resentment magically disappear." According to John Bean, Kate is tamed "not by a Petruchio's whip, but when she discovers her own imagination, for when she learns to recognize the sun for the moon and the moon for the dazzling sun she is discovering the liberating power of laughter and play." Yet they have been unable to account for the problem of closure because they separate Petruchio's modern, progressive, playful games from the willful, arbitrary, and tyrannical domination they associate with patriarchy. In separating coercion from role-playing, these critics are committed to the assumption that Petruchio will stop playing once he tames Kate, and this assumption presents them with a problem: why does Petruchio continue to play after Kate is transformed on the road to Padua? Why does the comedy continue after Kate wins Petruchio's wager?

We can begin to answer these questions if we see that Petruchio's role-playing does not oppose patriarchy but relocates and reinforces it within a domestic relationship; the husband increases his authority over his wife by gaining her love. The aim of Petruchio's games, as with the Protestant domestic courtesy literature to which *The Taming of the Shrew* is so often favorably compared, is less to create a relationship between equals based on reciprocal duties and obligations than it is to maintain patriarchal domination by emphasizing the importance of married love. In *The Family, Sex, and Marriage in England: 1500–1800*, Lawrence Stone observes that

> the Protestant sanctification of marriage and the demand for married love itself facilitated the subordination of wives. Women were now expected to love and cherish their husbands after marriage and were taught that it was their sacred duty to do so. This love, in those cases where it in fact became internalized and

> real, made it easier for wives to accept that position of submission to the will of their husbands upon which the preachers were also insisting. By a paradoxical twist, one of the first results of the doctrine of holy matrimony was a strengthening of the authority of the husband over the wife and an increased readiness of the latter to submit herself to the dictates of the former. Sir Kenelm Digby complacently remarked in the late 1630's that one should be careful to choose an obedient wife, "which none can promise to himself . . . whose will is not wholly in his power by love."

Rather than creating a relationship between equals, according to Stone, the demand for married love tended to reinforce a patriarchal, hierarchical relationship.

I want to suggest that this demand for married love is embedded in a discursive practice composed not only of conduct manuals and Protestant sermons but also of plays performed for the middle-class Protestant, London householders who made up a large segment of Shakespeare's audience. *The Taming of the Shrew*, in particular, displays the capacity of role-playing to reinforce patriarchy by intensifying the emotional bond between husband and wife. Petruchio wins Kate's love because his playfulness gives him an authority of an untraditional, imaginative, and irrational type, a type Weber termed "charismatic" (*Max Weber: The Interpretation of Social Reality*, edited by J. E. T. Eldridge). According to Weber, charismatic authority is irrational, emotional, and agonistic. Charisma "may involve a subjective or internal reorientation born out of suffering, conflicts or enthusiasm." Charismatic authority creates or demands new obligations and it must continually be reaffirmed because it is maintained outside the realm of everyday routine, outside of institutions. "The only basis for legitimacy for it," Weber says, "is personal charisma, so long as it is proved; that is, as long as it receives recognition and is able to satisfy the followers of disciples. But this lasts only so long as the belief in its charismatic inspiration remains." Thus, charismatic authority is occasional; it has to be constantly renewed, or, in the idiom of Renaissance, continually rehearsed.

By considering Petruchio's authority as charismatic, we can grasp the essential unity of features in his character which have hitherto seemed disparate or even contradictory. Petruchio's irreverent, untraditional, "mad" behavior at his wedding, his sometimes subversive mockery of Baptista, his saturnalian trip with Kate to his home, his willfulness, his combination of force (or the threat of force) and imaginative play, his interests in contests are all in the service of a new kind of patriarchal authority grounded not in an abstract and unchanging ideology of the wife's absolute and unquestioning obedience to her husband but on his ability to *display* that obedience. Petruchio's authority over Kate gains legitimacy as Kate willingly and even lovingly performs in front of an audience whatever Petruchio tells her to do or say. Thus, modern critics have been right to see that the primary aim of Petruchio's is not to curb Kate's "mad and headstrong humor" (4.1.211) through brute force but to gain her love. What they tend to deny, however, is that love and power are deeply connected. Petruchio's charismatic authority ultimately disguises the fact that his taming process is a coercive, social practice designed to discipline, control, and subordinate Kate. To be sure, at certain moments in the play, Petruchio does not directly dominate Kate: on the road to Padua when she and Petruchio encounter Vincentio, and in her final speech, she improvises willingly. But Petruchio's control over Kate seems to have been eliminated only because they found a common if momentary target of aggression, in the shape of Vincentio. Tensions within the domestic relationship cannot be entirely sublimated because Petruchio always maintains his authority by directing Kate; her performance is always a command performance. Domestic unity and social order are of course provisionally achieved, but only because aggression has been displaced, or, to put it another way, scapegoated; that is, social unity depends on a scapegoat, a victim, who enables Petruchio and Kate to unite by directing collective aggression at him.

Once we see that Petruchio's games are a means of establishing his charismatic authority, we can also understand the formal problem of closure. A resolution to social and domestic conflicts can never be conclusive, and coercion never finally disappears, because Kate's display of her obedience is always occasional; it must be repeated because it is demonstrated by a performance. Without a victim to use as a scapegoat, Petruchio's behavior towards Kate always becomes more overtly coercive behavior. The frame cannot return, I will argue, because it would call attention to the artificiality of the play, thereby disrupting its social function, namely, to disguise the fact that Petruchio can never cease to be coercive.

Petruchio's coerciveness is masked through a scapegoat mechanism. Petruchio and Kate become emotionally closer whenever Petruchio enables Kate to redirect the aggression he directs at her at another victim. The connection between domestic union and scapegoating can be seen most clearly at the moment critics believe is completely free of aggression and coercion—Kate's conversion on the road to Padua. When Kate initially submits to Petruchio she has not been tamed, as critics quite rightly point out, because she does so somewhat grudgingly:

> Then, God be blest, it is the blessed sun,
> But sun it is not, when you say it is not,

> And the moon changes even as your mind.
> What you will have it nam'd, even that it is,
> And so it shall be so for Katherine.
>
> (4.5.18–22)

Although Hortensio thinks that Petruchio has finally tamed Kate, exclaiming "Petruchio, go thy ways, the field is won" (4.5.23), it is only when Kate joins in Petruchio's playful transformations of reality that she is in fact tamed. When Kate jokingly refers to the sun as she asks Vincentio's pardon, we know she has joined in Petruchio's game:

> Pardon, old father, my mistaking eyes,
> That have been so bedazzled by the sun,
> That every thing seemeth green;
> Now I perceive thou art a reverent father.
> Pardon, I pray thee, for my mistaking.
>
> (4.5.45–49)

According to modern critics, Petruchio continues to be coercive, contradicting and berating Kate after she initially submits to him, not because he wants to dominate a submissive wife, as Hortensio seems to think, but because he wants to play with an independent and energetic woman who is an equal.

Yet coercive domination apparently gives way to playful liberation only because Petruchio and Kate are able to focus aggression on an outsider, Vincentio. Modern critics isolate Petruchio and Kate from the full dramatic context in which their union occurs. Kate's transformation, they assume, could occur at any given moment; it is essentially arbitrary. Kate is tamed when it finally dawns on her that Petruchio has been playing with her all along. Yet it is quite clear that her transformation is not, in fact, arbitrary; it depends on the presence of another human being, Vincentio. The sun and moon are not sufficient objects of play to unite Kate and Petruchio; that is, before Vincentio comes on stage, Petruchio and Kate are only superficially reconciled; Kate submits to Petruchio only because she does not want to return to his home. Yet once Vincentio enters, Petruchio and Kate unite. Why? Domestic union depends on channeling aggression away from Kate onto a third person outside the relationship. The union Petruchio and Kate achieve in this scene comes at Vincentio's expense: as a stranger, Vincentio is a common target of their play; he remains baffled and amazed while they pretend he is a budding virgin. Coercion temporarily disappears only because Kate manages to redirect aggression away from herself and at Vincentio.

Petruchio is more directly coercive at later moments in the play when a common target is unavailable. Critics are often disturbed when Petruchio threatens to return home after Kate initially refuses to kiss him:

> KATHERINA: Husband, let's follow to see the end of this ado.
> PETRUCHIO: First kiss me Kate, and we will.
> KATHERINA: What in the midst of the street? . . .
> PETRUCHIO: Why then let's home again. Come, sirrah, let's away.
> KATHERINA: Nay, I will give thee a kiss; now pray thee, love, stay.
> PETRUCHIO: Is not this well? Come, my sweet Kate:
> Better once than never, for never too late.
> (5.1.143–45; 147–50)

Petruchio's threat may seem superfluous and even cruel. Robert Heilman argues, for example, that

> when Petruchio asks a kiss, we do have human beings with feelings, not robots; but the key line in the scene, which is sometimes missed, is Petruchio's "Why then let's home again. Come sirrah, let's away" (5.1.146). Here Petruchio is again making the same threat that he made at 4.5.8–9, that is, not playing an imaginative game but hinting the symbolic whip, even though the end is a compliance she is inwardly glad to give.

Yet Petruchio compels a kiss from Kate because they do not have a common target. Coercion has not been necessary up to this point because Petruchio and Kate have detached themselves from the "ado" (5.1.142) Lucentio's secret and unauthorized marriage to Bianca has created. Even though Petruchio and Kate do not actively mock Vincentio or the other characters, they can stand aside and watch the action as spectators together. When they are alone, however, Petruchio once again resorts to coercion, and threatens, as Heilman puts it, the symbolic whip.

The ideological relation between comic form and the coerciveness of Petruchio's role-playing now becomes apparent. The *Shrew* does not end on the road to Padua or when Lucentio and Bianca reveal that they have secretly married because a socially acceptable target of aggression has to be found to replace Vincentio: if social and domestic unity depends on a victim, a comic butt, not any victim will do. The aggression Petruchio and Kate direct at Vincentio is quietly subversive because he is a father; even though Petruchio and Kate hardly do more than play a practical joke on him, they nevertheless take their joking seriously: Kate twice asks to be pardoned by the "reverent father" (4.5.49) she newly perceives and Petruchio seconds her request (4.5.49–50). The felt need for pardon is a powerful index not only of the aggressiveness of their play but also of its subversiveness.

It is this subversiveness that the resolution of *The Taming of the Shrew* attempts to manage and control. Domestic union consistently comes at the expense of obedience to parents and to fathers in particular. Although the play begins with the assumption that the father has complete authority over his daughters—Baptista being able to prevent the marriage of his younger daughter until the elder is married—the play continually challenges that authority. Lucentio and Bianca marry without Baptista's consent, and Vincentio is nearly jailed because Tranio refuses to admit that he is acting the part of Lucentio. Moreover, Petruchio's excessive and aggressively unconventional behavior is directly linked to his father's death. In response to Hortensio's inquiry, Petruchio explains that he has been blown to Padua by

> Such wind as scatters young men through the world
> To seek their fortunes farther than at home,
> Where small experience grows. But in a few,
> Signor Hortensio, thus it stands with me:
> Antonio, my father, is deceas'd,
> And I have thrust myself into this maze,
> Happily to wive and thrive it as best I may.
>
> (1.2.50–56)

Petruchio's sexual and imaginative impulses, linked by the word "thrust," his desire to "wive and thrive," are released only after his father has died. Petruchio's games and Lucentio's disguise affirm and reinforce the authority of the husband over the wife at the expense of the father's authority over his daughter.

The resolution of *The Taming of the Shrew* contains this subversiveness and reinforces domestic union by finding a socially acceptable target of aggression—women. Petruchio's wager, that is, licenses verbal and physical aggression against Bianca and the widow. Petruchio tells Kate that she may use force to make them come to their husbands if they are reluctant to do so:

> Go fetch them hither. If they deny to come,
> Swinge me them soundly forth unto their husbands.
> Away, I say, and bring them hither straight.
>
> (5.2.103–5)

More important, the wager licenses verbal aggression: Kate is able to chastise the women precisely because they have been disobedient, thereby taking an active role in Petruchio's games. Communal solidarity and domestic unity are not simply renewed and affirmed, then, but come at the expense of Bianca and the widow; women replace fathers as socially acceptable targets of collective aggression. The resolution cannot be achieved without victims. After Kate's final speech in defense of patriarchy, Bianca and the widow are silent. Men alone celebrate Kate's reformation.

The comic form of the *Shrew* is essentially ideological. Closure occurs when coercion has apparently been eliminated from Petruchio's role-playing by redirecting it unto other women. An obvious moment of closure would seem to occur when Kate wins Petruchio's wager for him by coming when he calls her. The fact that Petruchio continues to make demands on Kate disturbs critics because Lucentio and Hortensio have conceded that Petruchio has won, and Baptista has added twenty thousand crowns to Kate's dowry because he is so pleased. Yet Petruchio is not content:

> Nay, I will win my wager better yet,
> And show more sign of her obedience,
> Her new-built virtue and obedience.
> (5.2.116–18)

Why this need for such a public display of Kate's obedience? Why doesn't closure occur once Kate appears? Why doesn't it occur when Kate willingly throws under foot a highly significant material object, especially within Renaissance culture, her cap? Kate's willingness to do whatever Petruchio tells her to do would seem to demonstrate his mastery conclusively. The play does not end here because Petruchio still seems coercive. Until Kate is allowed to improvise her own speech in defense of patriarchy, Petruchio seems to be compelling her to prove her obedience. Every command he gives is aggressive, arbitrary, and willful, and the effect is to undermine the illusion that the play attempts to maintain, namely, that domestic union is independent of coercion. Petruchio does not invite Kate to come or to stomp on her cap, or suggest that she tell Bianca and the women their duty to their husbands: he commands her and she obeys.

The resolution effects a displacement of this aggression so that domestic union can be affirmed and intensified without apparent coercion when Kate takes the initiative and chastises away from herself and onto others just as she did on the road to Padua. Yet Petruchio is nevertheless still Kate's master: he charges her to "tell these headstrong women / What duty they owe their lords and husbands" (5.2.130–31) and he decides for her that she address the widow first. Kate's ability to improvise and extend her speech is only an illusion of freedom; Petruchio always controls and initiates the games.

Petruchio's wager succeeds, then, in reinforcing his right supremacy and in reinforcing patriarchy generally; for in the final moments of the play, the victims of Kate's play are not fathers, but women.

Because domestic harmony is achieved by displacing aggression inside the relationship towards others outside it, complete and conclusive social harmony cannot be achieved. The resolution does not put an end to social tensions and conflicts between characters, but keeps certain conflicts open in order to close others down; that is, domestic union between Petruchio and Kate depends on their difference from the other couples, a difference to which Petruchio joyfully calls attention:

> Come, Kate, we'll to bed.
> We three are married, but you two are sped.
> 'Twas I won the wager, though you hit the white,
> And being a winner, God give you good night!
>
> (5.2.184–87)

Petruchio's games provide a measure of social harmony and domestic intimacy because they are inconclusive; coercion seems to disappear only when he and Kate have aggressively differentiated themselves from Paduan society. The resolution depends further on a distinction between private and public space; the public wager and feast give way to the privacy of the bedroom.

If Petruchio's relationship with Kate is so deeply patriarchal, why, we may wonder, is it so compelling? Why do so many critics believe, despite clear evidence to the contrary, that the love between Petruchio and Kate is entirely separate from coercion? The relationship seems attractive in part because it seems so natural, as if Kate were just waiting for someone like Petruchio to come along and tame her. Petruchio's coercion is in the service of natural bodily impulses, and he abandons it in the final moments of the play because it is no longer necessary. Instead, Petruchio embraces Kate after she finishes her speech: "Why, there's a wench! Come on, and kiss me, Kate" (5.2.180). And Petruchio then invites Kate to bed.

The problem with the view that the play is a celebration of a natural relationship between a man and a woman, however, is that it implicitly makes one an apologist for patriarchy: what critics take to be natural turns out to be political. When Hortensio wonders what Kate's transformation bodes, Petruchio's reply links love and happiness to his mastery over Kate:

> Marry, peace it bodes, and love, and quiet life,
> An aweful rule, and right supremacy;
> And to be short, what not, that's sweet and happy.
>
> (5.2.108–10)

Peace, love, quiet, and happiness are inseparable from rule and supremacy. Without the disciplinary strategy Petruchio employs, domestic and social unity could not be achieved.

Love can never conclusively be separated from coercion because romantic love is not natural; it does not spring spontaneously from natural impulses but is rather the product of a disciplinary practice. If the love between Petruchio and Kate appears to be natural, it is because the play engineers that effect in order to legitimate Petruchio's power; that is, coercion is ultimately justified, even if it never entirely disappears, because it only affirms the natural order of things.

Yet *The Taming of the Shrew* pays a price to disguise Petruchio's coerciveness. Social and domestic harmony are achieved at the expense of formal coherence. Instead of complete and balanced dramatic closure, the *Shrew* ends without the frame returning. The disappearance of the frame has been interpreted in two contrary ways. In one interpretation, the frame's absence is taken to be a dramatic flaw. As Robert Heilman argues [in his introduction to the Signet edition]: "Surely most readers feel spontaneously that in the treatment of Sly something is left uncomfortably hanging." Other critics have argued less convincingly that the frame's disappearance doesn't matter because the play is unified as it is. In this account, the *Shrew*'s structure reinforces a series of moral distinctions between various kinds of play, implicitly differentiating Petruchio's role-playing from the Lord's and from Lucentio's on moral grounds: Petruchio plays seriously to effect a permanent transformation in Kate, while the Lord plays gratuitously and Lucentio plays only in order to win Bianca.

Both of these interpretations share the same assumption about formal unity: the play should be unified. To see dramatic form as ideological, however, is to see that the disappearance of the frame is symptomatic of the play's social function: were the frame to return, it would jeopardize the social function of the comedy. The moral distinctions between Petruchio's role-playing and the Lord's practical joking implied by the structure are never conclusively established, if only because the structure is equivocal: it invites us to compare the Lord and Petruchio as much as it enables us to differentiate them. The frame disappears partly because this equivocation cannot be sustained in the play's closing moments: the frame would undermine the ideological function of the play; by suggesting that the play is only a dream, only a play-within-a-play, the frame would heighten our sense of the artificiality of Petruchio's behavior at the very moment the play is at pains to naturalize it, to make us feel that Kate is from a dream newly waken. Thus, the frame would alienate the audience from the world of the play instead of engaging them.

Given the social purpose of the *Shrew*, it makes perfect sense that the play ends without the frame. For the point of naturalizing Petruchio's relationship with Kate is to impose the resolution on the audience, to enchant us and make us feel that Petruchio is an ideal husband and Kate an ideal wife. Kate's final speech is directed not only at Bianca and the widow, but at the women in the audience as well. Shakespeare makes use of the interplay between two kinds of theatrical space, the *platea* and *locus*, in order to break down any distinction between the play world on stage and the world of the audience. In his study of Shakespeare's complex interplay between platea and locus (*Shakespeare and the Popular Tradition in the Theater*), Robert Weimann argues that the platea is a neutral space which an actor uses to make a direct appeal to the audience while still remaining within the illusion of the play. Shakespeare makes use of the platea in Kate's speech, giving her defense of patriarchy a generality beyond its immediate dramatic occasion, in order to unite the world of the audience and the world of the play. Kate does not address only Bianca and the widow but women in general. She refers, for example, to "our bodies, soft, and weak, and smooth . . . our soft conditions, and our hearts" (5.2.165, 167). The generality and universality of Kate's speech are sustained by men who respond to Kate's speech in general terms. Vincentio remarks that " 'Tis a good hearing when children are toward" (5.2.182), while Lucentio replies in uncomfortable counterpoint "But a harsh hearing when women are toward" (5.2.183). In the final scene, laughter, pleasure, wonder, and the comic energies of the play all put us on the side of Petruchio and Kate, that is to say, on the side of patriarchal values.

It is tempting to see the *Shrew*'s lack of formal coherence as a means of alienating us from patriarchy, secretly inviting us to criticize it. Instead of reinforcing patriarchy, *The Taming of the Shrew* would, in this view, ironically undermine the resolution it apparently supports, demystifying the scapegoat mechanism at the heart of the social order. The temptation is strong because it saves the text from an ideology we find disagreeable, to say the least. I have been concerned to show, however, that the formal problems of the play are produced precisely because the text is itself a form of ideological production. Shakespeare does not stage the subversion of patriarchy but stages a subversive threat to patriarchy—the unruly and insubordinate woman—in order to contain it. The lack of formal unity evidences a desire to manage potential sources of subversion rather than a desire to subvert the social order.

To say that Shakespeare's comic form is shaped by the coercive function of his comedies is not to say that they are flawed or unliterary; rather, it is to revise our sense of what is characteristically Shakespearean about them. Modern critics tend to view comedies which seem too obviously artificial and coercive either as failures or as problem plays. *The Two Gentlemen of*

Verona is a failure because its ending is arbitrarily forced on a plot over which Shakespeare seems to have lost control. Similarly, *All's Well That Ends Well* and *Measure for Measure* are viewed as problem plays because the playwright (or a surrogate playwright such as Duke Vincentio) forces the comic resolution. Only in the so-called "mature" comedies are the resolutions fully harmonious, free of coercion or clumsiness. *The Taming of the Shrew* is often marked off from the mature comedies as an early farce, a failed romantic comedy, because men initiate and control the games; in the mature comedies, women and men are liberated from conventional constraints through role-playing and word-play.

The force of my reading of the *Shrew* is not simply to suggest that every Shakespearean comedy is a problem comedy; it is to understand that the resolutions are always problematic because every comedy is the site of conflicting interests and forces. If in the mature comedies, women and men seem more free, it is not because coercion is absent; rather, the cunning of the later comedies lies in the way they disguise their coerciveness by subjecting men and women to the same disciplinary strategies. The point will be clearer if we turn to *Much Ado about Nothing*, a play rightly considered to be a revision of *The Taming of the Shrew*. Like the *Shrew, Much Ado* celebrates the idea that love is natural; as Benedick puts it, "The world must be peopled" (2.3.242). Yet the resolution of *Much Ado* is far from harmonious. The reunion between Claudio and Hero seems forced and unrealistic largely because it does not fully redeem Claudio from his earlier, inexcusable public humiliation of Hero. The need for coercion is more explicit in the central relationship between Beatrice and Benedick. The marriage ceremony is interrupted when Beatrice unveils herself because it is unclear if Beatrice and Benedick are actually in love. Their union is saved only by the intervention of Leonato and Claudio:

> BENEDICK: Do you not love me?
> BEATRICE: Why, no; no more than reason.
> BENEDICK: Why, then your uncle and the prince and Claudio
> Have been deceiv'd; they swore you did.
> BEATRICE: Do you not love me?
> BENEDICK: Troth, no, no more than reason.
> BEATRICE: Why then my cousin Margaret and Ursula
> Are much deceiv'd, for they did swear you did.
> BENEDICK: They swore you were almost sick for me.
> BEATRICE: They swore you were well-nigh dead for me.
> BENEDICK: 'Tis no such matter. Then you do not love me?

> BEATRICE: No, truly, but in friendly recompense.
> LEONATO: Come, cousin, I am sure you love the gentleman.
> CLAUDIO: And I'll be sworn upon't that he loves her.
>
> (5.4.74–85)

The resolution does not turn on the conclusive revelation of a deeply felt bond but instead radically calls into question the notion that Beatrice and Benedick have been hiding their true feelings for each other from themselves and from their friends and relatives. The sonnets Claudio and Leonato produce as evidence of love between Beatrice and Benedick are inconclusive, since the sonnets were written after the deceptions practiced on them by their friends began. The difference between *Much Ado about Nothing* and *The Taming of the Shrew* is not that *Much Ado* is less coercive, more enlightened in its representation of heterosexual union; rather, the difference is that *Much Ado* locates coercion in social and communal interests outside the lovers themselves. The mature comedies can apparently be differentiated from the problem comedies only because some comedies mask their coerciveness more effectively than others. Problem comedies such as *Measure for Measure* reveal more explicitly what is always the case in Shakespearean comedy: comic resolutions are the product of force.

The Turn of the Shrew

Joel Fineman

HORTENSIO: *Now go thy ways, thou has tam'd a curst shrow.*
LUCENTIO: *'Tis a wonder, by your leave, she will be tam'd so.*
(5.2.188–89)

In ways which are so traditional that they might be called proverbial, Shakespeare's *Taming of the Shrew* assumes—it turns out to make no difference whether it does so ironically—that the language of woman is at odds with the order and authority of man. At the same time, again in ways which are nothing but traditional, the play self-consciously associates this thematically subversive discourse of woman with its own literariness and theatricality. The result, however, is a play that speaks neither for the language of woman nor against the authority of man. Quite the contrary: at the end of the play things are pretty much the same—which is to say, patriarchally inflected—as they were at or before its beginning, the only difference being that now, because there are more shrews than ever, they are more so. It cannot be surprising that a major and perennially popular play by Shakespeare, which is part of a corpus that, at least in an English literary tradition, is synonymous with what is understood to be canonical, begins and ends as something orthodox. Nevertheless, there is reason to wonder—as my epigraph, the last lines of the play, suggests—how it happens that a discourse of subversion, explicitly presented as such, manages to resecure, equally explicitly, the very order to which it seems, at both first and second sight, to be opposed. This question, raised by the play in a thematic register, and posed practically by the play by virtue of the play's historical success, leads to another: is it possible to voice a language, whether of man or of woman, that does not speak,

From *Shakespeare and the Question of Theory*, edited by Patricia Parker and Geoffrey Hartman.

sooner or later, self-consciously or unconsciously, for the order and authority of man?

Formulated at considerably greater levels of generality, such questions have been advanced by much recent literary, and not only literary, theory, much of which finds it very difficult to sustain in any intelligible fashion an effective critical and adversary distance or difference between itself and any of a variety of master points of view, each of which claims special access to a global, universalizing truth. It is, however, in the debates and polemics growing out of and centering upon the imperial claims of psychoanalysis that such questions have been raised in the very same terms and at precisely the level of generality proposed by *The Taming of the Shrew*—the level of generality measured by the specificity of rubrics as massive and as allegorically suggestive as Man, Woman, and Language—for it is psychoanalysis, especially the psychoanalysis associated with the name of Jacques Lacan, that has most coherently developed an account of human subjectivity which is based upon the fact that human beings speak. Very much taking this speech to heart, psychoanalysis has organized, in much the same ways as does *The Taming of the Shrew*, the relationship of generic Man to generic Woman by reference to the apparently inescapable patriarchalism occasioned by the structuring effects of language—of Language, that is to say, which is also understood in broad genericizing terms. In turn, the most forceful criticisms of psychoanalysis, responding to the psychoanalytic provocation with a proverbial response, have all been obliged, again repeating the thematics of *The Taming of the Shrew*, to speak against this Language for which the psychoanalytic speaks.

Thus it is not surprising, to take the most important and sophisticated example of this debate, that Jacques Derrida's (by comparison) very general critique of logocentric metaphysics, his deconstructive readings of what he calls the ontotheological ideology of presence in the history of the west, turns more specifically into a critique of phallogocentric erotics in the course of a series of rather pointed (and, for Derrida, unusually vociferous) attacks on Lacanian psychoanalysis. Lacan serves Derrida as a kind of limit case of such western "presence," to the extent that Lacan, centering the psychology of the human subject on a lack disclosed by language, deriving human desire out of a linguistic want, is prepared to make a presence even out of absence, and, therefore, as Derrida objects, a God out of a gap. As is well known, Derrida opposes to the determinate and determining logic of the language of Lacan—though with a dialectic that is of course more complicated than that of any simply polar opposition—an alternative logic of *différance* and writing, associating this a-logical logic with a "question of style" whose status as an irreducible question keeps alive, by foreclosing any univocal answer, the deconstructive power of a corresponding "question of woman." Here again, however, it is possible to identify the formulaic ways in which this Derridean alternative to a psychoanalytic logos recapitulates, because it predicates itself as something Supplementary and Other, the general thematics of *The Taming of the Shrew*. And this recapitulation has remained remarkably consistent, we might add, in the more explicitly feminist extensions of the deconstructive line traced out by Derrida, all of which, for all the differences between them, attempt to speak up for, and even to speak, a different kind of language than that of psychoanalytic man (e.g., the preverbal, presymbolic "semiotic" of Julia Kristeva, the *écriture féminine* of Hélène Cixous, the intentionally duplicitous or bilabial eroticism of Luce Irigaray, the Nietzschean narcissism of Sarah Kofman).

This theoretical debate between psychoanalysis and the deconstructive feminisms that can be called, loosely speaking, its most significant other is in principle interminable to the extent that psychoanalysis can see in such resistance to its Language, as Freud did with Dora, a symptomatic confirmation of all psychoanalytic thought. In the context of this debate, *The Taming of the Shrew* initially possesses the interest of an exceptionally apt literary example, one to which the different claims of different theories—about language, desire, gender—might be fruitfully applied. On the other hand, to the extent that this debate appears itself to reenact the action that is staged within *The Taming of the Shrew*, there exists the more than merely formal possibility that the play itself defines the context in which such debate about the play will necessarily take place. Understood in this way, the theoretical quarrel that might take place about *The Taming of the Shrew* would then emerge as nothing more than an unwitting reproduction of the thematic quarrel—between Man and Woman or between two different kinds of language—that already finds itself in motion in *The Taming of the Shrew*. If this were the case—and it remains to determine with what kind of language one might even say that this is the case—then the self-conscious literariness of *The Taming of the Shrew*, the reflexively recursive metatheatricality with which the play presents itself as an example of what it represents, would acquire its own explanatory, but not exactly theoretical, value. Glossing its own literariness, the play becomes the story of why it is the way it is, and this in turn becomes a performative account or self-example of the way a theoretical debate centered around the topoi of sexuality, gender, and language appears to do no more than once again repeat, to no apparent end, an old and still ongoing story.

That the story is in fact an old one is initially suggested by the ancient history attaching to the three stories joined within *The Taming of the Shrew*: the Christopher Sly framing plot, where a lord tricks a peasant into thinking himself a lord, which goes back at least as far as a fable in *The Arabian Nights*; the story of Lucentio's wooing of Bianca, which can be traced back, through Gascoigne and Ariosto, to Plautus or Menander; and the taming story proper, Petruchio's domestication of the shrewish Kate, which is built up out of innumerable literary and folklore analogues, all of which can claim an antique provenance. Correlated with each other by means of verbal, thematic, and structural cross-references, these three independent stories become in *The Taming of the Shrew* a single narrative of a kind whose twists and turns would seem familiar even on first hearing. Indeed, the only thing that is really novel about the plotting of *The Taming of the Shrew* is the way the play concatenates these three quite different stories so as to make it seem as though each one of them depends upon and is a necessary version of the other two.

Moreover, the play itself insists upon the fact that it retells a master plot of Western literary history. By alluding to previous dramatic, literary, and biblical texts, by quoting and misquoting familiar tags and phrases, by parodically citing or miming more serious literary modes (e.g., Ovidian narrative and Petrarchan lyric), the play situates itself within a literary tradition to which even its mockery remains both faithful and respectful. This is especially the case with regard to the taming subplot that gives the play its name. Soon after he enters, for example, Petruchio cites proverbial precursors for the cursing Kate, in one brief passage linking her not only to the alter ego of the Wife of Bath but also to the Cumaean Sibyl and Socrates' Xantippe (1.2.69–71) (these references later to be counterbalanced by Kate's translation to "a second Grissel, and Roman Lucrece" [2.1.295–96]). Such women are all touchstones of misogynistic gynecology. The commonplace way in which Petruchio evokes them here, drawing from a thesaurus of women whose voices will systematically contradict the dictates of male diction, is characteristic of the way, from beginning to end, the play works to give archetypal resonance and mythological significance to Kate's specifically female speech, locating it in the context of a perennial iconography for which the language of woman—prophetic and erotic, enigmatic and scolding, excessive and incessant—stands as continually nagging interference with, or as seductive and violent interruption of, or, finally, as loyally complicitous opposition to, the language of man.

What kind of language is it, therefore, that woman speaks, and in what way does it differ, always and forever, from the language of man? The first answer given by *The Taming of the Shrew* is that it is the kind of language Petruchio speaks when he sets out to teach to Kate the folly of her ways.

"He is more shrew than she" (4.1.85) summarizes the homeopathic logic of the taming strategy in accord with which Petruchio, assimilating to himself the attributes of Kate, will hold his own lunatic self up as mirror of Kate's unnatural nature. As perfect instance and reproving object lesson of his wife's excess, Petruchio thus finds "a way to kill a wife with kindness" (4.1.208). As an example which is simultaneously a counter-example, "He kills her in her own humour" (4.1.180). All Petruchio's odd behavior—his paradoxical and contradictory assertions, his peremptory capriciousness, his "lunacy," to use a word and image that is central to *The Taming of the Shrew*—presupposes this systematic and admonitory program of an eye for an eye, or, as the play defines the principle: "being mad herself, she's madly mated. / I warrant him, Petruchio is Kated" (3.2.244–45; "mated" here meaning "amazed" as well as "matched"). Moreover, all this madness bespeaks the language of woman, for Petruchio's lunatic behavior, even when it is itself nonverbal, is understood to be a corollary function, a derivative example, of the shrewish voice of Kate, as when Petruchio's horrific marriage costume, a demonstrative insult to appropriate decorum—"A monster, a very monster in apparel" (3.2.69–70)—is taken as a statement filled with a didactic sense: "He hath some meaning in his mad attire" (3.2.124).

In act 1, scene 2, which is the first scene of the taming subplot, Grumio, Petruchio's servant, explains the meaning as well as the method of Petruchio's madness. At the same time, he suggests how this is to be related to all the action, especially the verbal action, of the play:

> A' my word, and she knew him as well as I do, she would think scolding would do little good upon him. She may perhaps call him half a score knaves or so. Why, that's nothing; and he begin once, he'll rail in his rope-tricks. I'll tell you what, sir, and she stand him but a little, he will throw a figure in her face, and so disfigure her with it that she shall have no more eyes to see withal than a cat.
>
> (1.2.108–15)

This is an obscure passage, perhaps intentionally so, but "the general sense," as the editor of the Oxford edition says, "must be that Petruchio's railing will be more violent than Katherine's." Even so, it is the manner of the passage, more than its somewhat bewildering matter, that best conveys "the general sense" of Petruchio's project, a point brought out by the apparently unanswerable puzzle posed by "rope-tricks." On "rope-tricks" the Oxford editor says: "If emendation is thought necessary, 'rhetricks' is the best yet offered; but 'rope-tricks' may well be correct and may mean tricks that can be punished adequately only by hanging." The *Riverside* edition offers a similar answer to the "rope-tricks" question, but does so with even more uncertainty, as evidenced by the parenthetical question-marks that interrupt the gloss: "*rope-tricks*: blunder for *rhetoric* (an interpretation supported by *figure* in line 114(?) or tricks that deserve hanging(?)."

On the face of it, neither of these edgily tentative editorial comments is especially helpful in determining, one way or the other, whether Petruchio, when he "rails in his rope-tricks," will be doing something with language or, instead, performing tricks for which he should be hanged. The "interpretation," as the *Riverside* edition calls it, remains indeterminate. But such determination is of course not the point. The editors recognize—and so too, presumably, does an audience—that it is for what he does with language that Petruchio runs any risk with (bawdy) rope. Hence the special suitability of "rope-tricks" as a term to describe the way in which Petruchio will respond to Kate in verbal kind. Playing on "rhetoric" and on "rope," but being neither, "rope-tricks" simultaneously advances, one way *and* the other, both the crime (rape) and the punishment (rope) attaching to the extraordinary speech the play associates with Kate (rhetoric). "Rope-tricks," moreover, is a uniquely performative word for rhetoric, since "rope-tricks" *is* rhetoric precisely because it is not "rhetoric," and thus discloses, by pointing to itself, a kind of necessary disjunction between itself as a verbal signifier and what, as a signifier, it means to signify. In this way, as a kind of self-remarking case of rhetoric in action, "rope-tricks" becomes the general name not only for all the figurative language in the play but, also, for all the action in the play which seems literally to mean one thing but in fact means another: for prime example, the way in which Petruchio will speak the language of woman in order to silence Kate.

The point to notice about this is that, as far as the play is concerned, the "interpretation" of "rope-tricks," its meaning, is not altogether indeterminate or, rather, if it is indeterminate, this indeterminacy is itself very strictly determined. "Rope-tricks" is a word that univocally insists upon its own equivocation, and this definitive indeterminacy is what defines its "general sense." In a way that is not at all paradoxical, and in terms which are in no sense uncertain, the question posed by "rope-tricks" has as its answer the question of rhetoric, and the play uses this circularity—the circularity that makes the rhetoricity of a rhetorical question itself the answer to the question that it poses—as a paradigmatic model for the way in which, throughout the play, Petruchio will obsessively answer Kate with hysterical tit for hysterical tat.

Understood in this way, as "rope-tricks," we can say that the words and actions of *The Taming of the Shrew* rehearse a familiar antagonism, not simply the battle between the sexes but, more specifically, though still rather generally, the battle between the determinate, literal language traditionally spoken by man and the figurative, indeterminate language traditionally spoken by woman. But by saying this we are only returned, once again, to the question with which we began, for if such indeterminacy is what rhetoric always means to say, if this is the literal significance of its "general sense," why is it that this indeterminacy seems in *The Taming of the Shrew* so definitively to entail the domestication of Kate? Petruchio is never so patriarchal as when he speaks the language of woman—"He is more shrew than she"—just as Kate's capitulation occurs at the moment when she obediently takes her husband at his lunatic, female, figurative word. This happens first when Petruchio forces Kate to call the sun the moon, and then when Petruchio forces Kate to address a reverend father as "young budding virgin," a purely verbal mix-up of the sexes that leads an onlooker to remark: "A will make the man mad, to make a woman of him" (4.5.35–36). In accord with what asymmetrical quid pro quo does Petruchio propose to silence Kate by speaking the language she speaks, and why does the play assume that the orthodox order of the sexes for which it is the spokesman is reconfirmed when, madly translating a man into a mad woman, it gives explicit voice to such erotic paradox? Why, we can ask, do things not happen the other way around?

These are questions that bear on current theory. The editorial question-marks that punctuate the gloss on "rope-tricks" mark the same site of rhetorico-sexual indeterminacy on which Derrida, for example, will hinge his correlation of "the question of style" with "the question of woman" (this is the same disruptive question-mark, we can note, that Dora dreams of when she dreams about her father's death). But again, such questions are foregrounded *as* questions in *The Taming of the Shrew*, and in a far from naive manner. We learn, for example, in the very first lines of the play performed for Christopher Sly that Lucentio has come "to see fair Padua, the nursery of arts" (1.1.2), having left his father's "Pisa, renowned for grave citizens" (1.1.10). Lucentio's purpose, he says, is to "study / Virtue and that part of philosophy / . . . that treats of happiness" (1.1.17–19). This purpose stated, and the crazy psycho-geography of Padua thus established by its opposition to sober Pisa, Tranio, Lucentio's servant, then rushes to caution his master against too single-minded a "resolve / To suck the sweets of sweet philosophy" (27–28): "Let's be no Stoics nor no stocks," says Tranio, "Or so devote to Aristotle's checks / As Ovid be an outcast quite abjur'd" (31–32). Instead, Tranio advises his master to pursue his studies with a certain moderation. On the one hand, says Tranio, Lucentio should "Balk logic with acquaintance that you have," but, on the other, he should also "practice rhetoric in your common talk" (34–35). This is the initial distinction to which all the subsequent action of the play consistently and quite explicitly refers, a distinction that starts out as the difference between logic and rhetoric, or between philosophy and poetry, or between Aristotle and Ovid, but which then becomes, through the rhetorical question raised by "rope-tricks," the generalized and—for this is the point—quite *obviously* problematic difference between literal and figurative language on which the sexual difference between man and woman is seen to depend.

Tranio's pun on "Stoics"/"stocks," a pun which is a tired commonplace in Elizabethan comic literature, suggests both the nature of the problem and the way in which the play thematically exploits it. The pun puts the verbal difference between its two terms into question, into specifically rhetorical question, and so it happens that each term is sounded as the mimic simulation of the other. If language can do this to the difference between "Stoics" and "stocks," what can it do to the difference between "man" and "woman"? Is the one the mimic simulation of the other? This is a practical, as well as a rhetorical, question raised by the play, because the play gives countless demonstrations of the way in which the operation of stressedly rhetorical language puts into question the possibility of distinguishing between itself and the literal language it tropes. Petruchio, for example, when we first meet him, even before he hears of Kate, tells Grumio, his servant, to "knock me at the gate" (1.2.11). The predictable misunderstanding that thereupon ensues is then compounded further when a helpful intermediary offers to "compound this quarrel" (l. 27). These are trivial puns, the play on "knock" and the play on "compound," but their very triviality suggests the troubling way in which the problematic question raised by one word may eventually spread to, and be raised by, all. "Knock at the gate," asks Grumio, "O heavens! Spake you not these words plain?" (ll. 39–40).

Given the apparently unavoidable ambiguity of language or, at least, the everpresent possibility of such ambiguity, it is precisely the question, the rhetorical question, of speaking plainly that Grumio raises, as though one cannot help but "practice rhetoric" in one's "common talk." Moreover, as the play develops it, this argument between the master and his servant, an argument spawned by the rhetoricity of language, is made to seem the explanation of Kate's ongoing quarrel with the men who are her master. For example, the same kind of "knocking" violence that leads Petruchio and Grumio to act out the rhetorical question that divides them is what later leads Kate to break her lute upon her music-master's head: "I did but tell her she mistook her frets . . . And with that word she strook me on the head" (2.1.149–53).

Such "fretful" verbal confusions occur very frequently in the play, and every instance of them points up the way in which any given statement, however intended, can always mean something other than what its speaker means to say. For this reason, it is significant that, in almost the first lines of the play, Christopher Sly, after being threatened with "a pair of stocks" (Ind.1.2), explains not only why this is possibly the case but, really, why this is necessarily the case, formulating, in a "rope-trick" way, a general principle that accounts for the inevitability of such linguistic indeterminacy. "*Paucas pallabris*," says Christopher Sly, "let the world slide" (Ind. 1.5). The bad Spanish here is a misquotation from *The Spanish Tragedy*, Hieronimo's famous call for silence. An Elizabethan audience would have heard Sly's "*paucas pallabris*" as the comic application of an otherwise serious cliché, i.e., as an amusing deformation of a formulaic tag (analogous to Holofernes' "*pauca verba*" in *Love's Labor's Lost* [4.2.165]), whose "disfiguring" corresponds to the troping way in which Sly mistakenly recalls Hieronimo by swearing by "Saint Jeronimy" (Ind.1.9). So too with Sly's "let the world slide," which is equally proverbial, and which is here invoked as something comically and ostentatiously familiar, as something novel just *because* it sounds passé, being half of a proverb whose other half Sly pronounces at the end of the frame, in the last line of the induction, which serves as introduction to the play within the play: "Come madam wife, sit by my side, and let the world slip, we shall ne'er be younger" (Ind.2.142–43).

Taken together, and recognizing the register of self-parody on which, without Sly's knowing it, they seem to insist, the two phrases make a point about language that can serve as a motto for the rest of the play. There are always fewer words than there are meanings, because a multiplicity of meanings not only can but always will attach to any single utterance. Every word bears the burden of its hermeneutic history—the extended scope of its past, present, and future meanings—and for this reason every word carries with it a kind of surplus semiotic baggage, an excess of significance, whose looming, even if unspoken, presence cannot be kept quiet. Through inadvertent cognate homophonies, through uncontrollable etymological resonance, through unconscious allusions and citations, through unanticipatable effects of translation (*translatio* being the technical term for metaphor), through syntactic slips of the tongue, through unpredictable contextual transformations—in short, through the operation of "rope-tricks," the Word (for example, Sly's "world") will "slide" over a plurality of significances, to no single one of which can it be unambiguously tied down. Sly's self-belying cry for silence is itself an instance of a speech which is confounded by its excess meaning, of literal speech which is beggared, despite its literal intention, by an embarrassment of unintended semiotic riches. But the play performed before Sly—with its many malapropisms, its comic language lesson, its mangled Latin and Italian, its dramatic vivifications of figurative play, as when Petruchio bandies puns with Kate—demonstrates repeatedly and almost heavy-handedly that the rhetorical question raised by Grumio is always in the polysemic air: "Spake you not these words plain?"

It would be easy enough to relate the principle of "*paucas pallabris*" to Derrida's many characterizations of the way the everpresent possibility of self-citation—not necessarily parodic citation—codes every utterance with an irreducible indeterminacy, leaving every utterance undecidably suspended, at least in principle, between its literal and figurative senses. Even more specifically, it would be possible to relate the many proverbial ways in which the "wor(l)d" "slides" in *The Taming of the Shrew*—" 'He that is giddy thinks the world goes round' " (5.2.26), a proverb that can lead, as Kate remarks, to "A very mean meaning" (l. 31)—to Lacan's various discussions of the not so freely floating signifier. But, even if it is granted, on just these theoretical grounds, that the rhetoricity of language enforces this kind of general question about the possibility of a speaker's ever really being able to mean exactly what he means to say, and even if it is further granted that the "practice" of "rhetoric" in "common talk" is a self-conscious issue in *The Taming of the Shrew*, still, several other, perhaps more pressing, questions still remain. Why, for example, does the indeterminate question of rhetoric call forth the very determinate patriarchal narrative enacted in *The Taming of the Shrew*? Putting the same question in a theoretical register, we can ask why the question of rhetoric evokes from psychoanalysis the patriarchalism for which Lacan appears to be the most explicit mouthpiece, just as the same question provokes, instead, the antipatriarchal gender deconstructions—the chiasmically invaginated differences, the differentiated differences, between male and female—for which we might take Derrida to be the most outspoken spokesman.

To begin to think about these questions, it is necessary first to recognize that *The Taming of the Shrew* is somewhat more specific in its account of female language than I have so far been suggesting. For there is of course another woman in the play whose voice is strictly counterposed to the "scolding tongue" (1.1.252) of Kate, and if Kate, as shrew, is shown to speak a misanthropic, "fretful" language, her sister, the ideal Bianca of the wooing story, quite clearly speaks, and sometimes even sings, another and, at least at first, a more inviting tune. There are, that is to say, at least two kinds of language that the play associates with women—one good, one bad—and the play invents two antithetical stereotypes of woman—again, one good, one bad—to be the voice of these two different kinds of female speech.

This is a distinction or an opposition whose specific content is often overlooked, perhaps because Bianca's voice, since it is initially identified with silence, seems to speak a language about which there is not that much to say. Nevertheless, this silence of Bianca has its own substantial nature, and it points up what is wrong with what, in contrast, is Kate's vocal or vociferating speech. In the first scene of the play within the play, which is where we first meet these two women, Lucentio is made to be a witness to the shrewish voice of Kate—"That wench is stark mad or wonderful froward" (1.1.69)—and this loquacity of Kate is placed in pointed contrast to Bianca's virgin muteness: "But in the other's silence do I see / Maid's mild behavior and sobriety" (ll. 70–71). This opposition, speech versus silence, is important, but even more important is the fact that it is developed in the play through the more inclusive opposition here suggested by the metaphorical way in which Lucentio "sees" Bianca's "silence." For Bianca does in fact speak quite often in the play—she is not literally mute—but the play describes this speech, as it does Bianca, with a set of images and motifs, figures of speech, that give both to Bianca and to her speaking a specific phenomenality which is understood to be *equivalent* to silence. This quality, almost a physical materiality, can be generally summarized—indeed, generically summarized—in terms of an essential visibility: that is to say, Bianca and her language both are silent because the two of them are something to be *seen.*

One way to illustrate this is to recall how the first scene repeatedly emphasizes the fact that Lucentio falls in love with Bianca at first sight: "let me be a slave, t'achieve that maid / Whose sudden sight hath thrall'd my wounded eye" (1.1.219–20). A good deal of Petrarchan imagery underlies the visuality of Lucentio's erotic vision: "But see, while idly I stood looking on, /I found the effect of love in idleness" (1.1.150–51). More specifically, however, this modality of vision, this generic specularity, is made to seem the central point of difference between two different kinds of female language whose different natures then elicit in response two different kinds of male desire. There is, that is to say, a polar contrast, erotically inflected, between, on the one hand, the admirably dumb visual language of Bianca and, on the other, the objectionably noisy "tongue" (1.1.89) of Kate:

> TRANIO: Master, you look'd so longly on the maid . . .
> LUCENTIO: O yes, I saw sweet beauty in her face . . .
> TRANIO: Saw you no more? Mark'd you not how her sister
> Began to scold, and raise up such a storm
> That mortal ears might hardly endure the din?
> LUCENTIO: Tranio, I saw her mortal lips to move,

> And with her breath she did perfume the air.
> Sacred and sweet was all I saw in her.
>
> (1.1.165–76)

In *The Taming of the Shrew* this opposition between vision and language—rather, between a language which is visual, of the eye, and therefore silent, and language which is vocal, of the tongue, and therefore heard—is very strong. Moreover, as the play develops it, this is a dynamic and a violent, not a static, opposition, for it is just such vision that the vocal or linguistic language of Kate is shown repeatedly to speak against. In the first scene this happens quite explicitly, when Kate says of Bianca, in what are almost the first words out of Kate's mouth, "A pretty peat! It is best / Put a finger in the eye, and she knew why" (1.1.78–79). But this opposition runs throughout the play, governing its largest dramatic as well as its thematic movements. To take an example which is especially significant in the light of what has so far been said, we can recall that the "rope-tricks" passage concludes when it prophetically imagines Kate's ultimate capitulation in terms of a blinding cognate with the name of Kate: "She shall have no more eyes to see withal than a cat." Again, it is in terms of just such (figurative) blindness that Kate will later act out her ultimate subjection, not only to man but to the language of man: "Pardon old father, my mistaking eyes, / That have been so bedazzled with the sun . . . Now I perceive thou art a reverent father. / Pardon, I pray thee, for my mad mistaking" (4.5.45–49).

I have argued elsewhere that this conflict between visionary and verbal language is not only a very traditional one but one to which Shakespeare in his Sonnets gives a new subjective twist when he assimilates it to the psychology, and not only to the erotic psychology, of his first-person lyric voice. In addition, I have also argued that Shakespeare's different manipulations of this vision/language opposition produce generically different characterological or subjectivity effects in Shakespearean comedy, tragedy, and romance. It is far from the case, however, that Shakespeare invents this conflict between visual and verbal speech, for it is also possible to demonstrate that the terms of this opposition very much inform the metaphorical language through which language is imagined and described in the philosophico-literary tradition that begins in antiquity and extends at least up through the Renaissance, if not farther. While it is not possible to develop in a brief essay such as this the detailed and coherent ways in which this visual/verbal conflict operates in traditionary texts, it is possible to indicate, very schematically, the general logic of this perennial opposition by looking at the two rather well-known illustrations reproduced on pages 106 and 108. These pictures are by Robert Fludd, the seventeenth-century hermeticist, and they employ a thoroughly conventional iconography. A brief review of the two pictures will be worthwhile, for this will allow us to understand how it happens that a traditional question about rhetoric amounts to an answer to an equally traditional question about gender. This in turn will allow us to return not only to *The Taming of the Shrew* but also to the larger theoretical question with which we began, namely, whether it is possible to speak a Language, whether of Man or of Woman, that does not speak for the Language of Man.

The first picture, figure 1, is Fludd's illustration of the seventh verse of Psalm 63 (misnumbered in the picture as verse 8). "*In alarum tuarum umbra canam*," says or sings King David, and the picture shows precisely this. King David kneels in prayer beneath an eyeball sun, while from out of his mouth, in line with the rays of theophanic light which stream down on him, a verse of psalm ascends up to a brightness which is supported, shaded, and revealed by its extended wings. Because King David is the master psalmist, and because the picture employs perennial motifs, it would be fair to say that Fludd's picture is an illustration of psalmic speech per se. In the picture we see traditional figurations of the way a special kind of anagogic language does homage to an elevated referent. This referent, moreover, represented as an eye which is both seeing and seen, is itself a figure of a special kind of speech, as is indicated by the Hebrew letters inscribed upon its iris. These letters—*yod, he, vau, he*—spell out the name of God, "*Jehova*," which is the "Name" in which, according to the fourth verse of the psalm, King David lifts up his hands: "Thus wil I magnifie thee all my life, and lift up mine hands in the Name." However, though these letters spell out this holy name, nevertheless, in principle they do not sound it out, for these are letters whose literality, when combined in this famous Tetragrammaton, must never be pronounced. Instead, in accord with both orthodox and heterodox mystical prohibitions, this written name of god, which is the only proper name of God, will be properly articulated only through attributive periphrasis, with the letters vocalized either as *Adonai*, "the Lord," or as *Ha Shem*, "the Name" or even "the Word."

In Fludd's picture, where the verse of psalm and "*Jehova*" lie at oblique angles to each other, it is clearly the case that King David does not literally voice the name of God. It is possible, however, reading either up or down, to take inscribed "*Jehova*" as an unspoken part of David's praising speech, either as its apostrophized addressee or as the direct object of its "*canam*." This syntactic, but still silent, link between the Latin and the Hebrew is significant, for unspeakable "*Jehova*" thus becomes the predicated precondition through which or across which what the psalmist says is translated into what the psalmist sees. The picture is concerned to illustrate the effect of this translation, showing David's verse to be the medium of his immediate vision

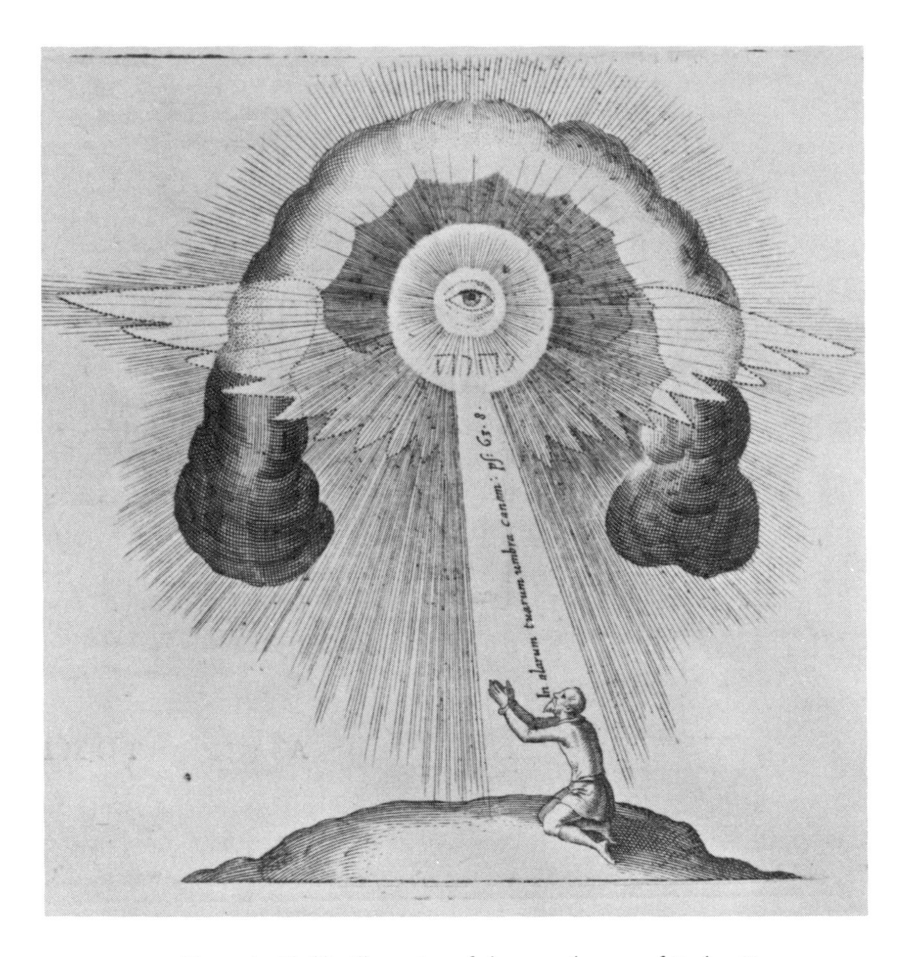

Figure 1: Fludd's illustration of the seventh verse of Psalm 63

of the sun, drawing David's verse as though it were itself a beam of holy light. In this way, because the verse is pictured as the very brightness that it promises to sing or speak about, Fludd's picture manages to motivate its portrait of a genuinely visionary speech. In the psalm, the reason why the psalmist praises is the very substance of his praise: "For thy loving kindnes is better then life: therefore my lippes shal praise thee." The same thing happens in the picture, where we see the future tense of "*canam*" rendered present, and where the promise of praise amounts to the fulfillment of the promise. But again, all this visionary predication depends upon the odd graphesis of unspeakable "*Jehova*," which is the signifier of all signifiers that even King David cannot bring himself to utter, just as it is the writing on his iris that even Jehova cannot read.

In an elementary etymological sense—remembering that "ideal" comes from Greek "*idein*," "to see"—Fludd's picture is a portrait of ideal language, of language that is at once ideal and idealizing. As the picture shows it, King David speaks a visual speech, a language *of* vision that promotes a vision *of* language, a language which is of the mouth only in so far as it is for the eye. This visual and visionary logos is nothing but familiar. Psalmic speech in particular and the language of praise in general (and it should be recalled that up through the Renaissance *all* poetry is understood to be a poetry of praise) are regularly imagined through such visual imagery, just as the referential object of such reverential praise is regularly conceived of as both agent and patient of sight. (Dante's vision of *luce etterna* at the end of the *Paradiso* would be a good example, though here again the height of vision is figured through a transcendental darkness, when power fails the poet's "*alta fantasia,*" and the poet's "will and desire" then "turn" ["*volgeva*"] with "the love that moves the sun and the other stars.")

In the second picture, Figure 2, which is by no means a strictly Elizabethan world picture (since its details go back at least to Macrobius and, therefore, through Plotinus, to Plato) we see the idealist aesthetics, metaphysics, and cosmology traditionally unpacked from and attaching to this visual idealism or visual idealization of the Word. As the title indicates, all arts are images of the specularity of integrated nature because both art and nature reciprocally will simulate the *eidola* or likenesses of beatific light. This commonplace eidetic reduction, which, by commutation, enables representation iconically to replicate whatever it presents, is what makes both art and nature into psalmic panegyric. Art becomes an art of nature just as nature is itself a kind of art, because they both reflect, but do not speak, the holy name which is the signifier and the signified of art and nature both. From this phenomenologically mutual admiration, which makes of art and nature each other's *special* (from *specere*, "to look at") likeness, it is easy to derive the ontotheological imperatives that inform all visionary art, for example, the poetics of *ut pictura poesis* and "speaking picture." Suspended from the hand of God, the great chain of mimetic being (which Macrobius describes as a series of successive and declensive mirrors) reaches down to nature, and through her to man, the ape of nature, whose artful calibration of a represented little world produces a demiurgic *mise en abyme* that in no way disturbs—indeed, one whose recursive reflections do nothing but confirm—the stability of the material world on which the ape of nature squats.

Not surprisingly, Fludd's encyclopedic picture of the hierarchic cosmos also includes a representation of a corresponding gender hierarchy. We can see this by looking at the circle of animals where, on the left, the picture illustrates generic man or *Homo* with his arms unfolded towards the sun,

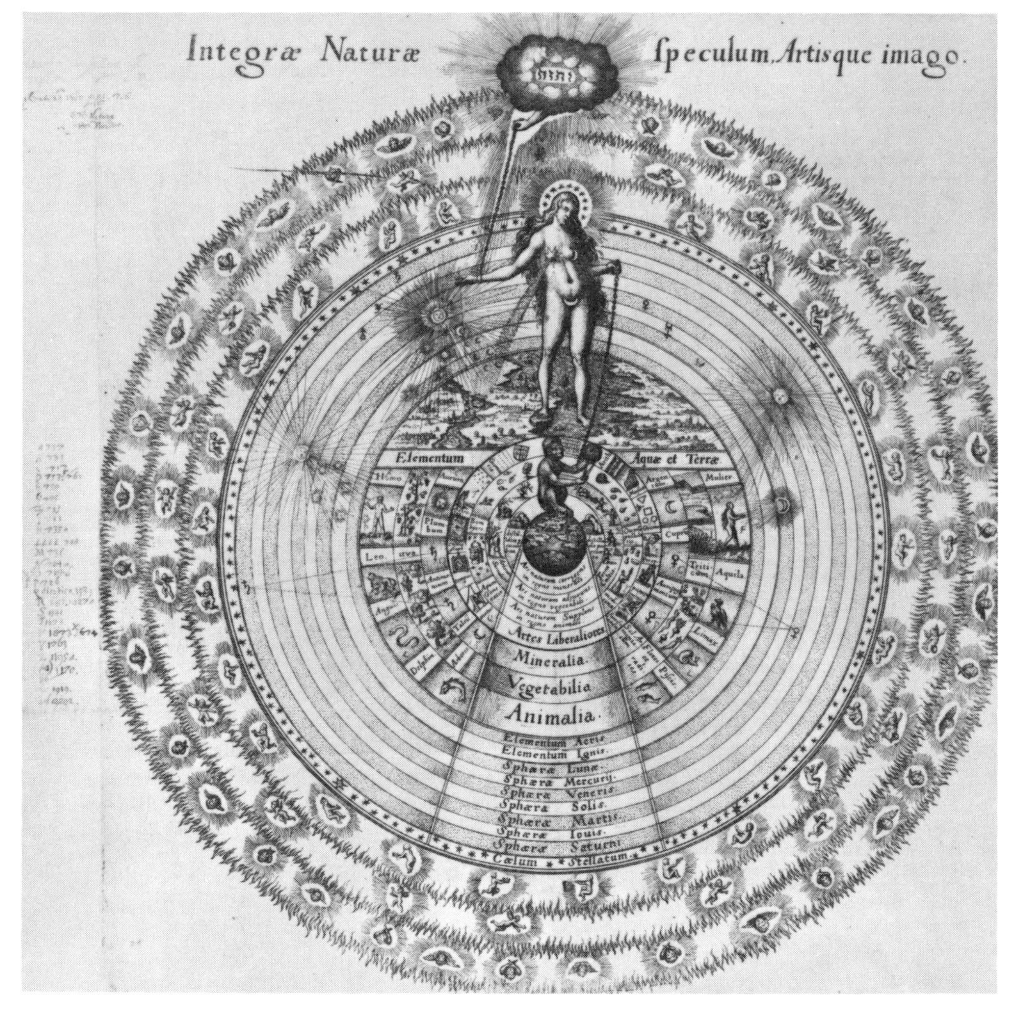

Figure 2: Fludd's encyclopedic picture of the hierarchic cosmos

in complementary contrast to the way that woman or *Mulier*, at the right of the circle of animals, looks instead up to the moon which is the pale reflection of the sun that shines above it. It is fair to say that this opposition, which makes woman the mimetic simulacrum of man, sketches out the horizontal gender opposition on which the vertical, metaphysical hierarchy of the cosmos perpendicularly depends. For this reason, however, it is important to notice that, as the picture shows it, this is not a simple or a simply polar contrast. Man is figured by the sun which is always the same as itself, whereas woman is figured by a waxing-waning-changing moon which is always other than itself, because its mimic light of likeness is what illuminates its difference from the sameness of the sun. Perhaps this constitutes a paradox, this lunar light which folds up likeness into difference. But if so, it is a paradox that stands in service of an orthodox erotics for which woman is the other to man, the hetero- to *Homo*, precisely because her essence is *to be* this lunatic difference between sameness and difference. In the same conventional way (conventional, certainly, at least up through Milton) that the difference between the sun and the moon *is* the moon, so too, and equally traditionally, the difference between man and woman is woman herself. This is a piety, moreover, that we see fleshed out in the ornaments of nature, who sports, with all decorum, a sun on one breast, a moon on the other, and, as the castrated and castrating difference between them, a second fetishistic moon upon her beatific crotch. Such is the erotics that is called for by traditional metaphysics. The word whose solar brightness is revealed by that which clouds it bespeaks a female darkness which is veiled by lunar brightness. The sickle-crescent moon of nature, which is cut and cutting both at once, indicates a mystery beyond it which is complementary to the way the odd graphesis of "*Jehova*" is constitutively eccentric to the centered wholeness of the world.

I have put this point in this way so as to point up the fact that there is really only one way to read Fludd's picture, and this precisely because there are two ways to read it. As with "rope-tricks," indeterminacy here again determines a specific story. On the one hand, given a set of assumptions about mimesis that go back at least to Plato, woman is the subordinate sub-version of originary man, in the same way that the moon is nothing more than an inferior reflection of the sun. In this sense, woman is nothing other than the likeness of a likeness. On the other hand, woman is equally the radical subversion of man, an insubordinate sub-version, because this system of mimesis inexorably calls forth a principle of difference which, as difference, is intrinsically excessive to such hierarchic likeness. In this sense, as the embodiment of difference—as, specifically, the difference *of* likeness—woman is nothing other than the other itself. The point to recognize, however, is not simply that these two hands go happily together—the logic of sub-version logically entailing its own subversion, the "Mirror of Nature" already displaying what Luce Irigaray will call the *speculum de l'autre femme*—but, more important, that the necessity of this double reading is no esoteric piece of wisdom. Quite the contrary; what we see in Fludd's picture is that this is a profoundly orthodox paradox, one whose formal heterogeneity, whose essential duplicity, is regularly figured and expressed by commonplace placeholders of the difference between sameness and difference, as, for example, unspeakable "*Jehova*," whose circumlocutory logos tangentially straddles the inside and the outside of the universal wholeness, or the titillating hole between the legs of nature whose absent presence is highlighted by discretionary light.

What Fludd's picture shows us, therefore, is that traditional iconography regularly assumes, as though it goes necessarily without saying, that there cannot be a picture of visionary language which is not at the same time an emblem of the limits of vision. This limit, however, as a limit, is built into Fludd's Wittgensteinian picture theory of language, within it as precisely that which such a theory is without. "*Jehova*," for example, is a part of *because* it is apart from the ideal specularity of the praising integrated world, and so too with the secret private parts of nature, whose hole we here see integrated into the deep recesses of nature's integrated whole. Out of this internal contradiction, figured through such motivating motifs, there derives, therefore, a very traditional story about the way the language of ideal desire is correlated with a desire for an ideal language. We see this story outlined in the circle of minerals, where man is associated with *Plumbum*, lead, and where woman is associated with *Cuprum*, named for the copper mines in Cyprus, birthplace of Venus, the goddess of love. Here we are to assume an alchemical reaction whereby Venus, the "Cyprian Queen," at once the object and the motive of desire, as a kind of catalytic converter, translates lead into gold, thereby supernaturally changing sub-nature into super-nature. And we can put this point more strongly by asserting that what Fludd's picture depicts is the thoroughly conventional way in which a universe of logical sameness is built up *on* its logical contra-diction (or, as it is sometimes written nowadays, as though this were a feminist gesture, its "cuntra-diction," i.e., the language of woman) because it is the very lunacy of discourse that returns both man and woman to the golden, solar order of the patriarchal Word.

At this level of allegorical generality, we can very quickly turn back to *The Taming of the Shrew* and understand how it happens that Petruchio reestablishes the difference between the sexes by speaking the lunatic language of woman. The language of woman *is* the difference between the sexes, a difference Petruchio becomes when, speaking "rope-tricks," he is "Kated." And this translation is dramatically persuasive because the play fleshes it out by invoking the sub-versive, subversive terms and logic of traditional iconography. In the taming story, the first moment of Kate's capitulation occurs when Petruchio, changing his mind, forces Kate first to call the sun the moon and then again the sun: "Then God be blest, it is the blessed sun, / But sun it is not, when you say it is not; / And the moon changes even as your mind. / What you will have it nam'd, even that it is, / And so it shall be so for Katherine" (4.5.18–22). We can call Kate's articulation of "change" the naming of the shrew which is the instrument of her taming, for it is this transcendentalizing, heliotropic, ontotheological paradox of "change"—"Then God be blest"—that leads Kate then to beg a patriarchal pardon for her blind confusion of the sexes: "Pardon, old father, my mistaking eyes, / That have been so bedazzled with the sun." And the same thing happens at the climax of the wooing story, when Lucentio, until then disguised as Cambio, kneels down before his father and reveals his proper self. "Cambio is chang'd into Lucentio" (5.1.123) is the line with which this revelation is theatrically announced. This formula serves to return the father and his son, along with the master and his servant, back to their proper order. But it also offers us an economical example of the way in which the very operation of rhetorical translation serves to change "change" into light.

To say that this paradox is orthodox is not to say that it describes a complete logical circle. Quite the contrary, as is indicated by the aporetic structure of Fludd's pictures, it is *as* a logical problem for logic, as an everpresent, irreducible, and ongoing question raised by self-reflection, that the paradox acquires its effective power. This is the question consistently raised by the insistent question of rhetoric, which is why, when Kate is tamed and order restored, the heretofore silent and good women of the play immediately turn into shrews. The subversive language of woman with which the play begins, and in resistance to which the movement of the play is predicated, reappears at the end of the play so that its very sounding predicts the future as a repetition of the same old story. This is the final moral of *The Taming of the Shrew*: that it is not possible to close the story of closure, for the very idea and idealization of closure, like the wholeness of Fludd's comprehensive cosmos, is thought through a logic and a logos whose internal disruption forever defers, even as this deferment elicits a desire for, a summary conclusion.

Hence, we can add, the function of the larger frame. Speaking very generally—and recalling, on the one hand, the Petrarchan idealism of the wooing story and, on the other, the parodic Petrarchanism, the Petruchioism, of the taming story—we can say that the two subplots of *The Taming of the Shrew* together present what in the Western literary tradition is the master plot of the relation between language and desire. Sly, however, to whom this story is presented, wishes that his entertainment soon were over, for only when the play is over will Sly get to go to bed with new-found wife. "Would 'twere done!" (1.1.254), says Sly (these being the last words we hear from him), of a play which, as far as Sly is concerned, is nothing but foreplay. The joke here is surely on Sly, for the audience knows full well that the consummation Sly so devoutly desires will never be achieved; if ever it happens that Sly sleeps with his wife, he will soon enough discover that she is a he in drag disguise. This defines, perhaps, the ultimate perversity of the kinky lord who "long[s] to hear" his pageboy "call the drunkard husband" (Ind.1.133), and who arranges for Sly to be subjected in this tantalizing way to what for Sly is nothing but the tedious unfolding of the play within the play. But it is not only Sly's desire that is thus seductively frustrated; and this suggests the presence, behind the play, of an even kinkier lord. I refer here to the ongoing editorial question regarding the absence of a final frame; for this response to the play's apparent omission of a formal conclusion to the Sly story is evidence enough that the audience for the entirety of the play is left at its conclusion with a desire for closure that the play calls forth *in order* to postpone. To say that this is a desire that leaves something to be desired—a desire, therefore, that will go on and on forever—goes a good way towards explaining the abiding popularity of *The Taming of the Shrew*.

Perhaps this also explains why, at first glance, it looks as though the current theoretical controversy to which I have referred presents us with a lovers' quarrel in which psychoanalysis plays Petruchio to its critics' Kate. It is tempting to see in the debate between Lacan and Derrida, for example, a domestic and domesticating quarrel that re-enacts in an increasingly more sophisticated but, for this reason, an increasingly more hapless fashion a proverbial literary predicament. However, this is not the conclusion that I would like to draw from the fact that current theoretical polemic so faithfully shapes itself to traditional literary contours and so voraciously stuffs itself with traditional literary topoi. Again it would be possible to relate the logic of sub-versive subversion, as it appears in Fludd and Shakespeare, to Derrida's gnostic, a-logical logic of the copulating supplement. And again, and again even more specifically, it would be possible to relate all this to Lacan's account of "The function and field of speech and language in psychoanalysis." Lacan's characterization of the relation of the imaginary to the symbolic very straightforwardly repeats the motifs of a traditional verbal/visual conflict, and it does so in a way that fully incorporates into itself its equally traditional intrinsic deconstruction, e.g., when Lacan says that the real is that which cannot be represented. When Lacan says, to take just a few examples, that the being of the woman is that she does not exist, or that the function of the universal quantifier, by means of which man becomes the all, is thought through its negation in woman's not-all, when he says that there is no sexual relation, or when he says that castration, the $-\phi$, is what allows us to count from 0 to 1, he is not only evoking the elementary paradox displayed in Fludd's picture—the class of all classes that do not classify themselves—he is also ornamenting this familiar paradox with its traditional figurative clothing. Thus it is that Lacan, like Derrida, is a master of the commonplace, as when he says that there is no such thing as metalanguage, or that "*La femme n'existe pas*," or that "*Si j'ai dit que le langage est ce comme quoi l'inconscient est structuré, c'est bien parce que le langage, d'abord, ça n'existe pas. Le langage est ce qu'on essaye de savoir concernant la fonction de la langue.*"

To recognize the fact that all of this is commonplace is to see that the argument between Lacan and Derrida, between psychoanalysis and its other (an argument that already takes place within Lacan and within psychoanalysis), repeats, not only in its structure but also in its thematic and illustrative details, a master plot of literature. To see this is also to recognize that coarse generic terms of a magnitude corresponding to that of man, woman, language historically carry with them an internal narrative logic which works to motivate a story in which every rubric gets to play and to explain its integrated role. At this level of generality it goes without saying that the language of woman inexorably speaks for the language of man, and it is therefore not surprising that a feminist critique of psychoanalysis which is conducted at this level of generality will necessarily recathect the story that is fleshed out in *The Taming of the Shrew*. If "Cambio is chang'd into Lucentio," so too, for example, is "Cambio" changed into Luce Irigaray.

It is, however, the great and exemplary value of both Lacan and Derrida that in their quarrel with each other they do more than scrupulously restrict their readings of the central topoi of Western self-reflexive language to the level of generality appropriate to the register of allegorical abstraction called for by such massive metaphoremes and motifs. In addition, they recognize this level of generality for what it is: the logic of the literary word in the west. Doing so, they open up the possibility of an extraliterary reading of literature. In a specifically literary context, Shakespeare is interesting because in Shakespeare's texts (from Freud's reading of which, we should recall, psychoanalysis originally derives) we see how, at a certain point in literary history, allegorical abstractions such as man, woman, language—formerly related to each other in accord with the psychomachian dynamics which are sketched out in Fludd's pictures—are introduced into a psychologistic literature, thereby initiating a recognizably modern literature of individuated, motivated character. But the relation to literature is not itself a literary relation, and there is no compelling reason, therefore, especially with the examples of Lacan and Derrida before them, why readers or critics of master literary texts should in their theory or their practice act out what they read.

Chronology

1564	William Shakespeare born at Stratford-on-Avon to John Shakespeare, a butcher, and Mary Arden. He is baptized on April 26.
1582	Marries Anne Hathaway in November.
1583	Daughter Susanna born, baptized on May 26.
1585	Twins Hamnet and Judith born, baptized on February 2.
1588–90	Sometime during these years, Shakespeare goes to London, without family. First plays performed in London.
1590–92	*The Comedy of Errors*, the three parts of *Henry VI.*
1593–94	Publication of *Venus and Adonis* and *The Rape of Lucrece*, both dedicated to the Earl of Southampton. Shakespeare becomes a sharer in the Lord Chamberlain's company of actors. *The Taming of the Shrew*, *The Two Gentlemen of Verona*, *Richard III*, *Titus Andronicus.*
1595–97	*Romeo and Juliet, Richard II, King John, A Midsummer Night's Dream, Love's Labor's Lost.*
1596	Son Hamnet dies. Grant of arms to Shakespeare's father.
1597	*The Merchant of Venice*, *Henry IV*, *Part 1.* Purchases New Place in Stratford.
1598–1600	*Henry IV*, *Part 2*, *As You Like It*, *Much Ado about Nothing*, *Twelfth Night*, *The Merry Wives of Windsor*, *Henry V*, and *Julius Caesar.* Moves his company to the new Globe Theatre.
1601	*Hamlet.* Shakespeare's father dies, buried on September 8.
1601–2	*Troilus and Cressida.*
1603	Death of Queen Elizabeth; James VI of Scotland becomes James I of England; Shakespeare's company becomes the King's Men.
1603–4	*All's Well That Ends Well*, *Measure for Measure*, *Othello.*
1605–6	*King Lear*, *Macbeth.*
1607	Marriage of daughter Susanna on June 5.

1607–8	*Timon of Athens*, *Antony and Cleopatra*, *Pericles*, *Coriolanus.*
1608	Shakespeare's mother dies, buried on September 9.
1609	*Cymbeline*, publication of sonnets. Shakespeare's company purchases Blackfriars Theatre.
1610–11	*The Winter's Tale*, *The Tempest.* Shakespeare retires to Stratford.
1612–13	*Henry VIII*, *The Two Noble Kinsmen.*
1616	Marriage of daughter Judith on February 10. Shakespeare dies at Stratford on April 23.
1623	Publication of the Folio edition of Shakespeare's plays.

Contributors

HAROLD BLOOM, Sterling Professor of the Humanities at Yale University, is the author of *The Anxiety of Influence*, *Poetry and Repression*, and many other volumes of literary criticism. His forthcoming study, *Freud: Transference and Authority*, attempts a full-scale reading of all of Freud's major writings. A MacArthur Prize Fellow, he is general editor of five series of literary criticism published by Chelsea House. During 1987–88, he served as Charles Eliot Norton Professor of Poetry at Harvard University.

MARJORIE B. GARBER, Professor of English at Harvard University, is the author of *Dream in Shakespeare: From Metaphor to Metamorphosis* and *Coming of Age in Shakespeare.*

MARIANNE L. NOVY, Associate Professor of English at the University of Pittsburgh, has written numerous articles on Shakespeare.

RUTH NEVO is Professor of English at Hebrew University in Jerusalem. She is the author of *The Dial of Virtue*, *Comic Transformations in Shakespeare*, and *Tragic Form in Shakespeare.* She has also translated into English the *Selected Poems* of Chaim Nachman Bialik.

COPPÉLIA KAHN, Associate Professor of English at Wesleyan University, is the author of *Man's Estate: Masculine Identity in Shakespeare.*

JEANNE ADDISON ROBERTS is Professor of English at the American University in Washington. She is the author of *Shakespeare's English Comedy: The Merry Wives of Windsor in Context.*

CAROL F. HEFFERNAN is a member of the Department of English at Rutgers University.

RICHARD A. BURT teaches in the English Department at Arizona State University.

JOEL FINEMAN, Associate Professor at the University of California, Berkeley, is the author of *Shakespeare's Perjured Eye: The Invention of Poetic Subjectivity in the Sonnets* and of essays on Shakespeare and on literary theory.

Bibliography

Alexander, Peter. "The Original Ending of *The Taming of the Shrew*." *Shakespeare Quarterly* 20 (1969): 111–16.

Barber, C. L. *Shakespeare's Festive Comedy: A Study of Dramatic Form and Its Relation to Social Custom*. Princeton: Princeton University Press, 1959.

Bean, John C. "Comic Structure and the Humanizing of Kate in *The Taming of the Shrew*." In *The Woman's Part: Feminist Criticism of Shakespeare*, edited by Carolyn Ruth Swift Lenz, Gayle Greene, and Carol Thomas Neely, 65–78. Urbana: University of Illinois Press, 1980.

Bergeron, David. "The Wife of Bath and Shakespeare's *The Taming of the Shrew*." *University Review* 35 (1968–69): 279–86.

Berry, Ralph. *Shakespeare's Comedies: Explorations in Form*. Princeton: Princeton University Press, 1972.

Bradbrook, M. C. "Dramatic Role as Social Image: A Study of *The Taming of the Shrew*." *Shakespeare Jahrbuch* 94 (1958): 132–50.

———. *The Growth and Structure of Elizabethan Comedy*. London: Chatto & Windus, 1955.

Brown, John Russell. *Shakespeare and His Comedies*. 2d ed. London: Methuen, 1962.

Bullough, Geoffrey, ed. *Narrative and Dramatic Sources of Shakespeare*, vol. 2, *The Comedies, 1597–1603*. New York: Columbia University Press, 1968.

Burckhardt, Sigurd. *Shakespearean Meanings*. Princeton: Princeton University Press, 1968.

Champion, Larry. *The Evolution of Shakespeare's Comedy: A Study in Dramatic Perspective*. Cambridge: Harvard University Press, 1970.

Charlton, H. B. *The Taming of the Shrew*. Manchester: Manchester University Press, 1932.

Coghill, Nevill. "The Basis of Shakespearean Comedy." In *Shakespeare Criticism: 1935–1960*, edited by Anne Ridler. Oxford: Oxford University Press, 1970.

Colie, Rosalie L. *Shakespeare's Living Art*. Princeton: Princeton University Press, 1974.

Dash, Irene C. *Wooing, Wedding and Power: Women in Shakespeare's Plays*. New York: Columbia University Press, 1981.

Elam, Keir. *Shakespeare's Universe of Discourse: Language-Games in the Comedies*. Cambridge: Cambridge University Press, 1984.

Evans, Bertrand. *Shakespeare's Comedies*. Oxford: Clarendon, 1960.

Felperin, Howard. *Shakespearean Romance*. Princeton: Princeton University Press, 1972.

Freedman, Barbara. "Errors in Comedy: A Psychoanalytic Theory of Farce." In *Shakespearean Comedy*, edited by Maurice Charney, 233–43. New York: New York Literary Forum, 1980.

Frye, Northrop. "The Argument of Comedy." In *English Institute Essays*, edited by D. A. Robertson, Jr., 58–73. New York: Columbia University Press, 1949.

———. *A Natural Perspective: The Development of Shakespearean Comedy and Romance.* New York: Columbia University Press, 1955. Reprint. New York: Harcourt Brace & World, 1965.

———. *The Secular Scripture: A Study of the Structure of Romance.* Cambridge: Harvard University Press, 1976.

Goddard, Harold C. *The Meaning of Shakespeare.* Chicago: University of Chicago Press, 1951.

Gussenhoven, Sr. Frances, R. S. H. M. "Shakespeare's *Taming of the Shrew* and Chaucer's Wife of Bath: The Struggle for Marital Mastery." *Chaucerian Shakespeare: Adaptation and Transformation.* Medieval and Renaissance Monograph Series. Detroit: Fifteenth-Century Symposium, 1983.

Hamilton, A. C. *The Early Shakespeare.* San Marino: Huntington Library, 1967.

Hartwig, Joan. "Horses and Women in *The Taming of the Shrew*." *Huntington Library Quarterly* 45 (1982): 285–94.

Heilman, Robert B. "The Taming Untamed, or, The Return of the Shrew." *Modern Language Quarterly* 27 (1966): 147–61.

———. Introduction to *The Taming of the Shrew*. In *The Complete Signet Classic Shakespeare.* New York: New American Library, 1966.

Henze, Richard. "Role Playing in *The Taming of the Shrew*." *Southern Humanities Review* 4 (1970): 231–40.

Hibbard, George. "*The Taming of the Shrew*: A Social Comedy." In *Shakespearean Essays*, edited by Alwin Thaler and Norman Sanders. *Tennessee Studies in Literature* 2 (1964): 15–28.

Hosley, Richard. "Sources and Analogues of *The Taming of the Shrew*." *Huntington Library Quarterly* 27 (1964): 289–308.

Houk, R. A. "The Evolution of *The Taming of the Shrew*." *PMLA* 57 (1942): 1009–38.

Hunter, Robert Grams. *Shakespeare and the Comedy of Forgiveness.* New York: Columbia University Press, 1965.

Huston, J. Dennis. *Shakespeare's Comedies of Play.* New York: Columbia University Press, 1981.

Jayne, Sears. "The Dreaming of *The Shrew*." *Shakespeare Quarterly* 17 (1966): 41–56.

Kirsch, Arthur. *Shakespeare and the Experience of Love.* Cambridge: Cambridge University Press, 1981.

Krieger, Elliot. *A Marxist Study of Shakespeare's Comedies.* London: Macmillan, 1979.

Leggatt, Alexander. *Shakespeare's Comedy of Love*. London: Methuen, 1974.

MacCary, Thomas W. *Friends and Lovers: The Phenomenology of Desire in Shakespearean Comedy.* New York: Columbia University Press, 1985.

Martz, William J. *Shakespeare's Universe of Comedy.* New York: David Lewis, 1971.

Montrose, Louis Adrian. " 'The Purpose of Playing': Reflections on a Shakesperian Anthropology." *Helios*, n.s. 7 (1980): 51–74.

Muir, Kenneth. *Shakespeare's Comic Sequence.* Liverpool: Liverpool University Press, 1979.

Nelson, Thomas Allen. *Shakespeare's Comic Theory: A Study of Art and Artifice in the Last Plays.* The Hague: Mouton, 1972.

Ornstein, Robert. *Shakespeare's Comedies: From Roman Farce to Romantic Mystery.* Newark: University of Delaware Press, 1986.

Ranald, Margaret Loftus. "The Manning of the Haggard, or *The Taming of the Shrew.*" *Essays in Literature* 1 (1974): 149–65.

Ribner, Irving. "The Morality of Farce: *The Taming of the Shrew.*" In *Essays in American and English Literature Presented to Bruce Robert McElderry, Jr.*, edited by Max F. Shultz. Columbus: Ohio University Press, 1967.

Riemer, A. P. *Antic Fables: Patterns of Evasion in Shakespeare's Comedies:* New York: St. Martin's, 1980.

Righter, Anne. *Shakespeare and the Idea of the Play.* London: Chatto & Windus, 1962.

Roberts, Jeanne Addison. "Animals as Agents of Revelation: The Horizontalizing of the Chain of Being in Shakespeare's Comedies." In *Shakespearean Comedy*, edited by Maurice Charney, 79–96. New York: New York Literary Forum, 1980.

Rossiter, A. P. *Angel with Horns and Other Shakespeare Lectures.* Edited by Graham Storey. London: Longmans, 1961.

Salingar, Leo. *Shakespeare and the Traditions of Comedy.* Cambridge: Cambridge University Press, 1974.

Scott, William O. *The God of Arts: Ruling Ideas in Shakespeare's Comedies.* Lawrence: University of Kansas Publications, 1977.

Seronsy, Cecil C. " 'Supposes' as the Unifying Theme in *The Taming of the Shrew.*" *Shakespeare Quarterly* 14 (1963): 19–23.

Shroeder, J. W. "*The Taming of a Shrew* and *The Taming of the Shrew*: A Case Reopened." *Journal of English and Germanic Philology* 57 (1958): 424–43.

Swinden, Patrick. *An Introduction to Shakespeare's Comedies.* London: Macmillan, 1973.

West, Michael. "The Folk Background of Petruchio's Wooing Dance: Male Supremacy in *The Taming of the Shrew.*" *Shakespeare Studies* 7 (1974): 65–73.

Williamson, Marilyn L. *The Patriarchy of Shakespeare's Comedies.* Detroit: Wayne State University Press, 1986.

Wilson, John Dover. *Shakespeare's Happy Comedies.* Evanston, Ill.: Northwestern University Press, 1962.

Yates, Francis A. *Shakespeare's Last Plays: A New Approach.* London: Routledge & Kegan Paul, 1975.

Acknowledgments

"Dream and Structure: *The Taming of the Shrew*" by Marjorie B. Garber from *Dream in Shakespeare: From Metaphor to Metamorphosis* by Marjorie B. Garber, © 1974 by Yale University. Reprinted by permission of Yale University Press.

"Patriarchy and Play in *The Taming of the Shrew*" by Marianne L. Novy from *English Literary Renaissance* 9, no. 2 (Spring 1979), © 1979 by *English Literary Renaissance.* Reprinted with permission.

" 'Kate of Kate Hall' " by Ruth Nevo from *Comic Transformations in Shakespeare* by Ruth Nevo, © 1980 by Ruth Nevo. Reprinted by permission of Methuen & Co.

"Coming of Age: Marriage and Manhood in *The Taming of the Shrew*" (originally entitled "Coming of Age: Marriage and Manhood in *Romeo and Juliet* and *The Taming of the Shrew*") by Coppélia Kahn from *Man's Estate: Masculine Identity in Shakespeare* by Coppélia Kahn, © 1981 by the Regents of the University of California. Reprinted by permission of the University of California Press.

"Horses and Hermaphrodites: Metamorphoses in *The Taming of the Shrew*" by Jeanne Addison Roberts from *Shakespeare Quarterly* 34, no. 2 (Summer 1983), © 1983 by the Folger Shakespeare Library. Reprinted by permission of *Shakespeare Quarterly and the author.*

"*The Taming of the Shrew:* The Bourgeoisie in Love" by Carol F. Heffernan from *Essays in Literature* 12, no. 1 (Spring 1985), © 1985 by Western Illinois University. Reprinted by permission.

"Charisma, Coercion, and Comic Form in *The Taming of the Shrew*" by Richard A. Burt from *Criticism: A Quarterly for Literature and the Arts* 26, no. 4 (Fall 1984), © 1985 by Wayne State University Press. Reprinted by permission.

"The Turn of the Shrew" by Joel Fineman from *Shakespeare and the Question of Theory,* edited by Patricia Parker and Geoffrey Hartman, © 1985 by Joel Fineman. Reprinted by permission.

Index

Animal metaphors, 54, 57, 58–59, 60–61, 62, 63
Antony and Cleopatra (Shakespeare), 59
Apologie for Women, An (Heale), 73
Arabian Nights, The, as influence on *The Taming of the Shrew,* 5–6, 55, 96
Ars Amatoria (Ovid), 53
Ashley, Maurice, on Elizabethan marriage customs, 69
As You Like It (Shakespeare), 39, 56, 62

Baptista, 31, 32, 33, 42, 43, 44, 60, 66, 67, 68, 72, 74, 77, 82, 86; character of, 21, 57–58, 70–71, 72–73
Barton, Anne, 29
Bean, John, 81
Beauvoir, Simone de, *The Second Sex,* 43
Becon, Thomas, *The Boke of Matrymony,* 70, 72
Berry, Ralph, 30
Bettelheim, Bruno, *The Uses of Enchantment,* 57
Bianca, 3, 31, 42–44, 49, 56–58, 63, 66–67, 70–73, 85–86, 87, 89–90, 96; character of, 1, 22–23, 32, 39, 57, 102–3
Boccaccio, Giovanni, *The Decameron,* 55
Boke of Matrymony, The (Becon), 70, 72
Bradbrook, Muriel, and Elizabethan drama, 54, 76

Caillois, Roger, *Man, Play, and Games,* 14–15
Charismatic authority: of Petruchio, 82–83; Weber on, 82
Charlton, H. B., 53
Christian State of Matrimony, The (Coverdale), 74
Climax and resolution, in Shakespearean comedy, 79–80, 92
Clothing, symbolism of, in *The Taming of the Shrew,* 18–19
Coghill, Nevill, 68
Comedy of Errors, The (Shakespeare), 56
Coverdale, Miles, *The Christian State of Matrimony,* 74
Crisis of the Aristocracy 1558–1644, The (Stone), 25

Decameron, The (Boccaccio), 55
Derrida, Jacques, and interpretation of *The Taming of the Shrew,* 94–95, 99, 112–13
Description of England, The (Harrison), 71
Domestical Duties (Gouge), 75

Elizabethan drama: Bradbrook and, 54, 76; metamorphosis as theme in, 54
Elizabethan marriage customs: Ashley on, 69; Wright on, 67, 69

Family, Sex, and Marriage in England: 1500–1800, The (Stone), 81–82
Farce, *The Taming of the Shrew* as, 41, 44–45, 53

Feminist interpretation, of *The Taming of the Shrew,* 1–2, 9, 29–30, 43, 45, 93, 96, 102–3, 109, 113
Fludd, Robert, illustrations of Psalms by, 104–10, 111, 112, 113
Fool and His Sceptre, The (Willeford), 16
Frye, Northrop: on character of Katherine, 2; on Shakespearean comedy, 49, 53, 56, 79–80

Game, Petruchio's behavior interpreted as a, 13, 14–15, 16–18, 19, 21, 24, 30, 81, 86, 87
Gascoigne, George, *The Supposes,* 58, 61, 72
Gibbon, Charles, *A Work Worth Reading,* 69, 72
Girard, René, on Shakespearean comedy, 80
Goddard, Harold: on character of Christopher Sly, 2, 4; on character of Petruchio, 2, 4; on feminist interpretation of Shakespeare, 1; on feminist interpretation of *The Taming of the Shrew,* 1–2
Gouge, William, *Domestical Duties,* 75
"Great chain of being," and *The Taming of the Shrew,* 47, 54
Greer, Germaine, 30
Gremio, 35, 43, 44, 49, 59, 70, 71, 72, 75
Grumio, 17, 36, 37, 44, 46, 60, 97, 100, 102

Harrison, William, *The Description of England,* 71
Heale, William, *An Apologie for Women,* 73
Heilman, Robert B., 6, 85, 89
Henry VI, Part III (Shakespeare), 21
Hermaphroditism, as metaphor in *The Taming of the Shrew,* 62–63
Heroides (Ovid), 53
Hibbard, George, 43
Homo Ludens (Huizinga), 14
Horse, as image in *The Taming of the Shrew,* 54, 57, 58–59, 62–63
Hortensio, 43, 44, 47, 50, 57, 60, 61, 62, 64, 68, 77, 84, 86, 88
Huizinga, Johan, *Homo Ludens,* 14
Hunt, as metaphor in *The Taming of the Shrew,* 55, 63

Induction, as used in *The Taming of the Shrew,* 2, 4, 5, 6–7, 9, 30–31, 54, 55, 56, 66–67, 80, 89, 96, 111–12
Irony, Shakespeare's use of, 79, 90

Janeway, Elizabeth, *Man's World, Woman's Place,* 23

Katherine, 70, 75, 76, 77, 110; character of, 2, 4, 7, 8, 15–16, 18, 19–20, 22, 23–24, 24–25, 29, 31–32, 33–34, 37–39, 41, 43–44, 47, 48, 49–51, 80–81, 82–84, 96–97, 100, 102–3; compared to Sly, 41–42; Tranio on, 44
King Lear (Shakespeare), 21
Kyd, Thomas, *The Spanish Tragedy,* 5, 101

Lacan, Jacques, and interpretation of *The Taming of the Shrew,* 94, 102, 112–13
Language, as used in *The Taming of the Shrew,* 15–16, 18–20, 22, 23–24, 26, 30, 93, 94–98, 99–102, 103–5, 110–11, 113
Little Prince, The (Saint-Exupery), 17
Love, as theme in Shakespearean comedy, 48–49
Love's Labor's Lost (Shakespeare), 1, 27, 56, 101
Lucentio, 8, 14, 18, 19, 24, 33, 42, 43, 58, 62, 64, 65–66, 67, 73, 77, 85–86, 89, 96, 99, 103, 111; character of, 22

Maid's Metamorphosis, The, 54

Malcontent (Marston), 5
Man, Play, and Games (Caillois), 14–15
Man's World, Woman's Place (Janeway), 23
Marriage, as depicted in *The Taming of the Shrew,* 42–43, 45–47, 50–51, 65–66, 68–73, 77
Marston, John, *Malcontent,* 5
Measure for Measure (Shakespeare), 92
Merchant of Venice, The (Shakespeare), 56
Merry Jest of a Shrewd and Curst Wife Lapped in Morel's Skin, 59, 61, 69
Merry Wives of Windsor, The (Shakespeare), 56
Metamorphoses (Ovid), 54, 62
Metamorphosis: Ovid's use of, 54; as theme in Elizabethan drama, 54
Midsummer Night's Dream, A (Shakespeare), 8, 11, 20, 55, 56, 62
Montrose, Louis Adrian, on Shakespearean comedy, 80
Much Ado about Nothing (Shakespeare): 56; *The Taming of the Shrew* compared to, 91–92

Novy, Marianne, 81

Old Wives' Tale, The, (Peele), 54
Ovid, 100; as influence on Shakespeare, 53–54, 61, 62, 63, 96; use of metamorphosis by, 54. Works: *Ars Amatoria,* 53; *Heroides,* 53; *Metamorphoses,* 54, 62

Patriarchy: as treated in *The Taming of the Shrew,* 13, 16–17, 20–21, 22–23, 24, 25–26, 27, 41–43, 44–47, 48, 49–51, 81–83, 85–86, 87–88, 93–94, 95, 99, 109
Pericles, Prince of Tyre (Shakespeare), 55
Petruchio, 100; appearance of, at his wedding, 16, 17, 22, 24, 35, 44, 73–75, 97; behavior of, interpreted as a game, 13, 14–15, 16–18, 19, 21, 24, 30, 81, 86, 87; character of, 2, 8, 10–11, 30, 33–37, 43, 44–47, 50–51, 59–60, 70, 75–76, 80–81, 82–84, 86–87, 88, 96–97, 110; charismatic authority of, 82–83; as stereotype, 41
Preparative to Marriage (Smith), 25–26
Psalms, Fludd's illustrations of, 104–10, 111, 112, 113
Psychoanalytic interpretation, of *The Taming of the Shrew,* 94–95, 102, 112–13

Quiller-Crouch, Arthur, 29

Richard III (Shakespeare), 1

Saint-Exupery, Antoine de, *The Little Prince,* 17
Second Sex, The (Beauvoir), 43
Shakespeare, William: Goddard on feminist interpretation of works of, 1; Ovid's influence on works of, 53–54, 61, 62, 63, 96; use of irony by, 79, 90
Shakespeare and the Popular Tradition in the Theater (Weimann), 90
Shakespearean comedy: climax and resolution in, 79–80, 92; Frye on, 49, 53, 56, 79–80; Girard on, 80; love as theme in, 48–49; Montrose on, 80
Shaw, George Bernard, 29
Sly, Christopher, 18, 55, 80, 96, 99, 102, 111–12; character of, 2, 6, 7, 10–11, 101; Katherine compared to, 41–42; metamorphosis of, 54, 56
Smith, Henry, *Preparative to Marriage,* 25–26
Spanish Tragedy, The (Kyd), 5, 101
Stone, Lawrence: *The Crisis of the Aristocracy 1558–1644,* 25; *The Family, Sex, and Marriage in England: 1500–1800,* 81–82
Supposes, The (Gascoigne), 58, 61, 72

Taming of a Shrew, The (Anon.), as analogue to *The Taming of the Shrew,* 6, 59, 65, 66–67, 69, 72, 76
Taming of the Shrew, The: animal metaphors in, 54, 57, 58–59, 60–61, 62, 63; *The Arabian Nights* as influence on, 5–6, 55, 96; Barton on, 29; Bean on, 81; Berry on, 30; Charlton on, 53; climax of, 80–81, 86–87; Coghill on, 68; compared to *Much Ado about Nothing,* 91–92; Derrida and interpretation of, 94–95, 99, 112–13; epilogue omitted from, 6; as farce, 41, 44–45, 53; feminist interpretation of, 1–2, 9, 29–30, 43, 45, 93, 96, 102–3, 109, 113; Goddard on feminist interpretation of, 1–2; and "great chain of being," 47, 54; Greer on, 30; Heilman on, 6, 85, 89; hermaphroditism as metaphor in, 62–63; Hibbard on, 43; horse as image in, 54, 57, 58–59, 62–63; the hunt as metaphor in, 55, 63; induction device as used in, 2, 4, 5, 6–7, 9, 30–31, 54, 55, 56, 66–67, 80, 89, 96, 111–12; Lacan and interpretation of, 94, 102, 112–13; language as used in, 15–16, 18–20, 22, 23–24, 26, 30, 93, 94–98, 99–102, 103–5, 110–11, 113; marriage as depicted in, 42–43, 45–47, 50–51, 65–66, 68–73, 77; Novy on, 81; patriarchy as treated in, 13, 16–17, 20–21, 22–23, 24, 25–26, 27, 41–43, 44–47, 48, 49–51, 81–83, 85–86, 87–88, 93–94, 95, 99, 109; as play within a play, 2, 5; psychoanalytic interpretation of, 94–95, 102, 112–13; Quiller-Crouch on, 29; Shaw on, 29; stage success of, 30; structure of, 80–81; symbolism of clothing in, 18–19; *The Taming of a Shrew* (Anon.) as analogue to, 6, 65, 66–67, 69, 72, 76; West on, 30

Tell-Trothes New-Yeares Gift, 70, 72
Tempest, The (Shakespeare), 7, 11
Thousand and One Nights, The. See Arabian Nights, The
Titus Andronicus (Shakespeare), 53–54
Tranio, 8, 11, 42, 43, 57, 66, 70, 71, 74, 86, 99, 100; character of, 18, 21–22; on Katherine, 44
Twelfth Night (Shakespeare), 56
Two Gentlemen of Verona, The (Shakespeare), 1, 30, 39; dramatic failure of, 90–91

Uses of Enchantment, The (Bettelheim), 57

Venus and Adonis (Shakespeare), 53–54
Vincentio, 8, 18, 24, 38, 48, 50, 58, 61, 83–84, 90, 91; character of, 21; as victim, 84–85

Weber, Max, on charismatic authority, 82
Weimann, Robert, *Shakespeare and the Popular Tradition in the Theater,* 90
West, Michael, 30
Willeford, William, *The Fool and His Sceptre,* 16
Winter's Tale, The (Shakespeare), 7, 59
Work Worth Reading, A (Gibbon), 69, 72
Wright, Louis, on Elizabethan marriage customs, 67, 69